GOOD NEWS FOR BRUISED REEDS

MENTAL HEALTH & THE GOSPEL COMMUNITY

"We are spirit beings that have soul-personalities in physical bodies. Unfortunately, we are fallen and live with other fallen people in a fallen world. This worsens the fracture of our souls. Since the mind is a primary doorway to our souls, it is imperative that we guard it against the deterioration from initial doubts to disappointments, discouragements to despondency, and depression (when it becomes clinical) to suicidal thoughts. This book comprises testimonies of various people about their journeys, as well as handles for recovery and restoration of our souls from this darkness. I highly commend this book to all in search of mental health as well as for those ministering to them."

Daniel Foo
Senior Pastor
Bethesda Bedok-Tampines Church

"I used to be the kind of Christian who would say: 'just deal with it'. Thankfully it was God who dealt with me—and saved me from such naive thoughts and arrogant attitudes. Journeying with a number of close friends who suffered from depression, anxiety and other deep wounds has made me appreciate how broken this fallen world really is ... and allowed me to see the long-suffering shape of our Father's love. I pray that this book will do the same for all of us in the body of Christ."

Dev Menon
Pastor
Zion Bishan Bible-Presbyterian Church

"Reading these real-life accounts is extremely difficult, especially when I spend a moment imagining how life would be in the sufferers' shoes. What can make an unthinkable pain even harder? When someone has to go through it alone, struggling to be understood by others, and constantly under the crushing weight of shame. If proclaiming a Christ who entered our broken world is the call of the Church, we need a book like this to help us empathise and enter the worlds of those who are suffering in different ways because of mental health challenges."

Jacob Ng
Assistant Lead Pastor
Redemption Hill Church

"I am truly touched by reading the life stories of actual people facing mental health issues. This book highlights the need for both professional mental health care and the Body of Christ to step in, to help and journey with anyone (and not just believers) facing mental health issues, with understanding and patience, compassion and love."

Lindis Szto
Pastoral Staff
Bethesda Frankel Estate Church

"Be warned that you will be hearing voices in this book. Voices of those who battle with anxiety, depression, schizophrenia and suicidal tendencies; voices of those whose loved ones are struggling with mental illnesses; voices of caregivers who fell into guilt and despair; voices of ministers who fought with depression; voices of those who care to speak up for the strugglers. Most importantly, it contains a prophetic voice calling the Church to repent from her lack of knowledge, and to become a safe community for the mentally broken to experience healing and wholeness in Christ."

Rick Toh
Lead Pastor
Yio Chu Kang Chapel

"Painfully moving and brutally honest stories told by Christians who have suffered mental illness; by their loved ones who stood by them in those times of darkness; and by the church community who reached out and supported them, despite sometimes not knowing what to do or say. In my decades as a clinical psychologist both at IMH and at MSF, in working with people with mental disorders and deep intrapsychic pain, I am often reminded and humbled by how mental infirmities increase our awareness of our human limitations and drives our need for the Divine."

Vivienne Ng
Clinical Psychologist

GOOD NEWS FOR BRUISED REEDS

MENTAL HEALTH & THE GOSPEL COMMUNITY

Edited by
Jonathan Cho, Joanna Hor, Ng Zhi-Wen,
Nicole Ong, Bernice Tan, Ronald JJ Wong

GRACEWORKS

Mental Health & the Gospel Community

Copyright © 2019 Graceworks Private Limited

The copyright for individual essays will reside with the individual authors.

All rights reserved. No part of this publication may be reproduced, stored in a retrieval system, or transmitted, in any form or by any means, electronic, mechanical, photocopying, recording or otherwise, without the prior written permission of the authors, except in the case of brief quotations embodied in critical articles and reviews.

Published by Graceworks Private Limited
22 Sin Ming Lane
#04-76 Midview City
Singapore 573969
Tel: 67523403
Email: enquiries@graceworks.com.sg
Website: www.graceworks.com.sg

All Scripture quotations, unless otherwise noted, are taken from the *Holy Bible*, New International Version®. NIV®. Copyright © 1973, 1978, 1984, 2011 by International Bible Society. Used by permission of Zondervan. All rights reserved.

Scripture quotations marked "ESV" are taken from *The Holy Bible*, English Standard Version. Copyright © 2000; 2001 by Crossway Bibles, a division of Good News Publishers. Used by permission. All rights reserved.

Scripture quotations marked "NLT" are taken from the *Holy Bible*, New Living Translation, copyright ©1996, 2004, 2015 by Tyndale House Foundation. Used by permission of Tyndale House Publishers, Inc., Carol Stream, Illinois 60188. All rights reserved.

Scripture quotations marked "RSV" are taken from the Revised Standard Version of the Bible, copyright © 1946, 1952, and 1971 National Council of the Churches of Christ in the United States of America. Used by permission. All rights reserved worldwide.

Scripture quotations marked "NKJV" are taken from the New King James Version®. Copyright © 1982 by Thomas Nelson. Used by permission. All rights reserved.

Scripture quotations marked "AMP" are taken from the Amplified Bible, Copyright © 1954, 1958, 1962, 1964, 1965, 1987 by The Lockman Foundation. Used by permission.

Scripture quotations marked "NASB" are taken from the New American Standard Bible® (NASB), Copyright © 1960, 1962, 1963, 1968, 1971, 1972, 1973, 1975, 1977, 1995 by The Lockman Foundation. Used by permission. www.Lockman.org"

Cover Illustration: Emma Lee, Awaken Studios

ISBN: 978-981-14-2770-1

A CIP record for this book is available from the National Library Board, Singapore.

3 4 5 6 7 8 9 10 • 26 25 24 23 22 21 20 19

CONTENTS

Changing our Minds: A Theological Introduction
to Mental Illness. xi
Leow Wen Pin

Introduction. xix
The Publisher

Section 1 — WHEN THE DARKNESS DESCENDS

Breaking Black. 1
Mike Wong

Hope is Finding Beauty in Ashes. 11
Alivia Kan

Not "Taboo®". 19
George Khoo

Chasing Angels, Chasing Eternity. 29
Dayne Hor

Walking in the Path of Life. 34
Hui Chew

Finding God in the Dark. 42
Mak Kean Loong

When Depression Drove Me Away from God. 51
Ruth*

Hope for the Anxious Mind. 58
Shoni Duesling

Lessons from the Brink—Reflection. 67
Tan Soo-Inn

Section 2 — WALKING WITH THE WOUNDED

How God Saved My Schizophrenic Mother (and Me). . 73
Alice*
When I Realised He Had Anxiety. 78
Myer Wong
Helplessness of the Helper. 85
Sophie Cheng
He Ain't Heavy, He's My Brother. 90
Paul Yong
When A Hurting Person is Hurt by the Church. 97
Chua JH*
A Journey of Finding More Questions than Answers. . .102
Fern Leong
We Will Arise and Shine. 108
Janet Chan-Lee
Perspectives from a Wife. 115
Wong Moy Yin
Sharing the Journey—Reflection. 121
Jonathan Cho

Section 3 — WALKING TOWARDS THE LIGHT

Soul Care as Spiritual Practice. 127
Andre Tan
A Pastor's Confession: Press the "Pause" Button. 134
Chua Seng Lee
My Ten Black Years. 141
Tan Soo-Inn
Discernment to Heal. 147
Daniel Jesudason
The Discernment Shepherds Need—Reflection. 155
Ronald JJ Wong

Journeying with the Mentally Ill: A Christian
Perspective—Afterword........................160
   Daniel Fung

Acknowledgements............................167

Help Resources in Singapore....................169

* These names and others in the individual stories have been changed to maintain confidentiality.

CHANGING OUR MINDS: A THEOLOGICAL INTRODUCTION TO MENTAL ILLNESS

– *Theological Overview*[1] –

"Though this be madness,
yet there is method in it."
— Polonius (from Hamlet, William Shakespeare)

Introduction

Mental illness is a reality that the Church in Singapore cannot ignore. The second Singapore Mental Health Study (SMHS), conducted in 2016 by the Institute of Mental Health (IMH), showed that one in seven people had experienced a mental disorder in their lifetime (an increase from the one-in-eight ratio obtained from the first SMHS conducted in 2010). The three most prevalent disorders identified were major depressive disorder, alcohol abuse, and obsessive-compulsive disorder. A particularly troubling aspect of the survey's results was the large size of the "treatment gap", i.e. the number of people who did not seek help for their condition. It was more than 80 percent.[2]

---

1 The author would like to thank Su Xinyi, Kevin Chow, Esther Phua, Edwin Phua, and Seah Chiew Kwan for their insightful comments on an earlier draft of this chapter.

2 Institute of Mental Health. "Latest Nationwide Study Shows 1 in 7 People in Singapore Has Experienced a Mental Disorder in Their Lifetime," December 11, 2018. https://www.imh.com.sg.

Another piece of research conducted in 2015 by IMH—the Well-being of the Singapore Elderly (WiSE) study—showed that one in 10 seniors (i.e. older than 60 years of age) in Singapore had dementia.[3] Accompanying this statistic was a worrying rise in early-onset dementia in younger individuals.[4] The WiSE study also showed that caring for a person with dementia was psychologically challenging, with 46 percent of caregivers expressing significant distress, and 11 percent experiencing depression or anxiety.

In light of these statistics, the Church needs to learn to respond well to this reality, not just because mental illness is already the lived experience of many church members, but also since the inclusive call of Jesus' gospel extends to people with mental illnesses. Reading the many touching personal stories in this book will help guide Christians to respond with sensitivity.

At the same time, to complement this empathy, theological reflection upon the Bible, mental illness, and human experience must be undertaken to provide Christians with a pastoral worldview through which to understand and include people with mental illnesses. Such reflection must *challenge deficient ways of thinking about* mental illness, and *provide redemptive hope* for persons with mental illnesses. We will briefly consider these two dimensions in this short introductory chapter.

---

3   Institute of Mental Health. "Study Establishes Prevalence of Dementia among Older Adults in Singapore," March 25, 2015. https://www.imh.com.sg.

4   From 2011–2016, the National Neuroscience Institute's Neuroscience Clinic saw a fivefold increase in patients with young-onset dementia, cf. Ng, Desmond. "He's 48, and Already Grappling with Dementia," June 7, 2018. www.channelnewsasia.com.

Challenging Deficient Ways of Thinking about Mental Illness

In lay Christian circles, demonic possession is a common way to explain mental illness.[5] Yet, such a way of thinking is unbiblical. A careful reading of the four Gospels shows only one episode where demonic possession is linked to atypical behaviour—the story of the Gerasene demoniac (Matthew 8:28–34; Mark 5:1–20; Luke 8:26–39). However, even in that one episode, the typical biblical Greek verb for "being mad" (*mainomai*) is not used, and the audience is left to guess the character's mental state from his violent behaviour. Surely this one passage is not a strong proof text for linking mental illness with demonic possession!

In contrast, when one investigates all the instances in the New Testament where the word *mainomai* is used, a very different picture emerges. For instance, in John 10:20, *mainomai* is used in the same sentence as the Greek word for demon (*daimonion*). However, it is used there in an accusation made against Jesus by his opponents: "He has a demon, and he is mad; why listen to him?" (RSV). This pattern of exclusion using the language of madness is repeated in Acts 12:15 when the disciples disbelieve Rhoda's account that Peter had supernaturally escaped from prison and was now standing at their front door, and in Acts 26:24–25 where Festus charges Paul with insanity for proclaiming the gospel. Finally, in 1 Corinthians 14:23, Paul observes that speaking in tongues (a gift of the Holy Spirit) will look like madness to outsiders. In all these occurrences of the word *mainomai*, not only is mental illness not attributed to demonic possession, language which links the two is often used by people to suppress

---

5 Marcia Webb, "Toward a Theology of Mental Illness," *Journal of Religion, Disability & Health* 16.1 (2012): 50–52.

the gospel or to disregard God's works. This is a sobering thought as we reflect on how some Christians still continue to use such rhetoric today.

Another common way of thinking about mental illness associates it with sin or the lack of faith. We must be careful here: while *some* instances of mental disorder might be the result of sinful choices, the Church must avoid the naïve association of sin/faithlessness with *all* instances of mental illness. As the Christian clinical psychologist Marcia Webb observes, while "some might argue that [when] Biblical characters like Elijah or Naomi experience depression and anxiety, these experiences may still be sin, or a result of a lack of faith … it is, however, impossible to maintain this argument when we consider Christ in the Garden of Gethsemane."[6]

This simplistic association of mental illness with sin has not just been perpetuated by lay Christians. Heath Lambert, a professor of biblical counselling, in critiquing the early biblical counselling movement, observes that the movement initially sought to explain mental illness *primarily* in terms of sin, even with conditions such as manic-depression and schizophrenia. However, Lambert notes that this approach was insufficient and ignored the crucial role that human suffering played in mental illness, which later generations of biblical counsellors have sought to recover.[7] This point is made strongly in this present volume's many stories which illustrate the varied causes of mental illness. Finally, in my own ministry experience, the most common way of thinking about mental illness in Christian circles

---

6   Webb, "Toward a Theology of Mental Illness," 57–58.
7   Heath Lambert, *The Biblical Counseling Movement after Adams* (Wheaton, Illinois: Crossway, 2011), 49–66.

today is the medicalised model. This model views biological causes as the *sole* source of mental illness.[8] For example, the chemical-imbalance explanation for certain types of mental illness, continues to be popular in lay circles today despite ongoing controversy.[9] Such a model ignores the fact that mental illness diagnoses are also human constructs, meant to provide mental health professionals with a working framework for organising the complexity of human mental behaviour.[10] These behaviours may not always have straightforward biological explanations.

Of course, this is not to deny that mental illnesses often do have biological influences. However, a major problem with the medicalised model is that it ignores the significant role that a person's community plays in mental well-being.

As the eminent pastoral theologian and mental health professional John Swinton notes concerning dementia, "It is located within the interface between the *individual's* physicality and experience and the attitudes, values, presumptions and relational abilities of the individual's *community*" (italics added).[11] In other words, the medicalised model is problematic because it narrowly focuses on the individual, making mental illness entirely their problem.

---

8   As N. Haslam remarks, medicalizing represents mental illness as "the product of somatic aberrations outside the person's control and thus akin to disease. ... Biomedical understandings of mental disorder dominate contemporary psychiatry" ("Dimensions of Folk Psychiatry," *Review of General Psychology* 9.1 (2005): 38–39).

9   Anatasia Philippa Scrutton, "Is Depression a Sin or a Disease? A Critique of Moralizing and Medicalizing Models of Mental Illness," *Journal of Disability and Religion* 19.4 (2015): 300–301.

10   R. E. Kendell and A. Jablensky, "Distinguishing between the Validity and Utility of Psychiatric Diagnoses," *American Journal of Psychiatry* 160 (2003): 4–12.

In contrast, the stories in this volume help us to recognise the Church's role in the making—and redeeming—of mental illness.

Providing Redemptive Hope

Given the deficiencies of the preceding models, how might we as the Church move towards a biblical and pastorally helpful model for mental illness? As a first step, such a model must locate mental illness in the *complex fallenness of all of creation*. Mental illness is not a single thing. It can have many causes: an individual's life choices, their fallen biology, unfortunate circumstances, alienating communities and social structures, or even a combination thereof. Such an assertion demands that Christian communities exercise mindful care in knowing and loving people with mental illness. We must not rush to simplistic diagnoses. This is certainly a discipline that can be practised as one reads through the many stories in this present volume.

Such a redemptive model of mental illness also calls churches to exercise sober self-reflection in examining whether we ourselves have played a role in promoting mental illness. In this regard, a sad truth that should lead many churches to repentance is the fact that mental illness is increasingly common among pastors.[12] Thankfully, the opposite can also be true: churches have the potential to be redemptive communities that nurture mental wellbeing through the practice of love, sincere welcome, and mutual hospitality. As the founder of the inclusive L'Arche

---

11   John Swinton, *Dementia: Living in the Memories of God* (Grand Rapids, Michigan: Eerdmans, 2012), 108.
12   Stetzer, Ed. "The Church and Mental Health: What Do the Numbers Tell Us?," August 5, 2018. https://www.christianitytoday.com.

communities, Jean Vanier, reminds us, "To be a disciple is to say to those in need, 'I love you and want to be committed to you, in order to help you to be liberated from rejection, and find the appropriate help as together we move towards peace and love.'"[13]

Moreover, by seeing mental illness as part of creation's fallenness, mental illness is included in God's redemptive plan for creation, rather than being something outside of the Bible's concerns. God's redemptive work thus encompasses persons with mental illnesses, giving them true hope that is grounded in God's promise that they will be restored to complete wellness when Jesus comes again. A foretaste of that hope can also be experienced in the present through the healing community that the Church is called to be. Hence, while a person's biological cause of mental illness might not be *cured* in this lifetime, that person can through the Church receive *healing*, namely, "the emergence of meaning, transformation, and personal growth that may take place alongside cure, but which may also take place in its absence."[14]

Persons with mental illnesses can therefore participate in God's redemptive plan as "wounded healers" (following Henri Nouwen).[15] As people who themselves have known the depths of human struggle, they themselves can minister to others using a profound compassion that emerges out of the common experience of pain. Hence, people

---

13 Jean Vanier and John Swinton, *Mental Health: The Inclusive Church Resource* (Darton, South Yorkshire: Longman & Todd, 2014), 63.

14 Anatasia Philippa Scrutton, "What Might It Mean to Live Well With Depression?," *Journal of Disability and Religion* 20.3 (2016): 179.

15 Henri J. M. Nouwen, *The Wounded Healer: Ministry in Contemporary Society* (New York, New York: Image, 1979).

with mental illnesses should not be regarded as helpless recipients of charity, but Spirit-empowered disciples capable of service. They can serve well, not just *despite* their illness, but even *because* of their illness. Their lives can breathe hope into the beating heart of the Church. Thus, they are indispensable to the Church.

This pattern of the "wounded healer" finds its perfect image in Jesus. He is the Healer who himself suffered the stigma of madness (John 10:20), yet whose wounds healed his people (1 Peter 2:24). For every person with mental illness, the person of Jesus reminds them that they have a God who intimately knows their pain. For them, he is their tender Saviour—"a bruised reed he will not break, and a dimly burning wick he will not quench" (Isaiah 42:3, RSV). So, though we walk the path of suffering now, we can look forward to the day when we will join him at his side, where "he will wipe away every tear from [our] eyes, and death shall be no more, neither shall there be mourning nor crying nor pain any more, for the former things have passed away" (Revelation 21:4, RSV). Until that day comes, may we follow our Saviour's example in softly tending to the tears of our precious brothers and sisters with mental illnesses.

Leow Wen Pin
Visiting Fellow
Biblical Graduate School of Theology

INTRODUCTION

"Feeling felt." This was a psychotherapeutic concept that I heard mentioned in a recent sermon on being known by God in Psalm 139. It struck a chord in me. It encapsulated how we should be privileged to feel in our relation both to God and with one another.

On further reading, I found this description of the phenomenon:

> *"Feeling felt" implies empathy paired with acceptance and presence. It engenders not only understanding, but also resonance. Two people sharing a sacred and respectful space. Being there together, without judgment, pressure, or agenda.*[1]

This is something that we in the gospel community should be offering to one another. More so, this is what we should be offering to those whose challenges—physical, mental, emotional—incapacitate them and cause them to feel excluded from society at large and the gospel community in particular.

If we believe that God is sovereign over all of life, the corollary would be that all come under His loving care. Which is why it is so comforting and important for us to

---

1   Partners in Healing. *Resonant Listening and the Power of "Feeling Felt"*. Accessed on 1 September 2019. https://www.partnersinhealingpsychotherapy.com/blog/resonant-listening-and-the-power-of-feeling-felt/ .

remember Isaiah 42:3–4. Not just for who Christ is, but for who we should be as we seek to be Christian. In one way or another, we are all bruised reeds.

Slightly more than a year ago, we published the first volume in the *Good News for Bruised Reeds* series. That volume addressed the bruised reeds among us who struggle with same-sex attraction. This prepared the way for opening up conversations among those who are struggling, those who care for them, and those in the gospel community who want to be better Christ lights to this community. As a result, many have experienced the nourishing effect of "feeling felt" and many leaders within the gospel community are beginning to work at life-giving change within their spheres of influence and friendship.

As we worked on publishing that first volume, one of the refrains that was constantly heard informed us of the numbers who experienced various mental health challenges. On a wider societal level, reports were also surfacing that reinforced our niggling thoughts that this is an area that needs to be brought into the light and not left to fester in the dark. The second Singapore Mental Health Study which was released in 2018 indicated that the lifetime prevalence of all mental disorders had shown an increase. "1 in 7 people in Singapore, has experienced a mood, anxiety or alcohol use disorder in their lifetime."[2]

It didn't take very much for the editorial team to agree that our second volume in the *Good News for Bruised Reeds* series should focus on mental health. This book

---

2   Institute of Mental Health. *Media Release* (Singapore: Institute of Mental Health, 11 December 2018).

you hold in your hand, *Mental Health & the Gospel Community*, has been birthed from our personal experiences that both within and without the gospel community those facing mental health challenges find the going aggravated by the misconceptions and sometimes theologically unsound assumptions made. Rather than "feeling felt", they feel condemned and ostracised because they cannot "snap out of it". It is time to begin a new set of conversations; ones that will be life-giving, will be empathetic and will not break the bruised reeds nor snuff out the smouldering wicks.

Those facing mental health challenges share their stories with us in Part 1. They paint for us the depths of personal anguish and, sometimes, even self-loathing as a result of their Sisyphean task of achieving a breakthrough. The voices you hear in Part 2 are shared by those who have walked with friends and loved ones. These caregivers' struggles are no less real as they support and agonise alongside the sufferers. Part 3 shows us that mental health challenges know no boundaries, and that pastors are not spared the worst of these challenges. However, having known the loneliness and struggles, these wounded healers now seek to be catalysts of change—to begin conversations that will bring Christ's healing love into the lives of those who suffer.

May our lives inspire the question for which Christ is the answer.

The Publisher

SECTION 1 — WHEN THE DARKNESS DESCENDS

BREAKING BLACK

*"*4:44 a.m."—a good title for the horror movie that I felt I was living in for a few months in 2016, when I was consistently overcome with panic attacks at that hour. Deep chest burns tore up my sleep. The feeling of irrational doom shrouded me. I'd sit in the bathroom for an hour, ask God for forgiveness for my sins and to take away the anxiousness and palpitations, and wait for the worst to pass.

I told a friend about my 4:44 a.m. episodes and he jokingly said, "It means die, die, die!" (when you say those numbers in Chinese).

I laughed but could not help wonder if it was a bad omen of some kind.

The Black Hole of Anxiety
I'd had nocturnal panic attacks on and off for years, and had been given medication to alleviate it. They often happened when life became very busy, like during Easter and Christmas when I had to direct plays in church. My church friends usually tried to make sense of it by calling it a spiritual attack, and attempted to pray it away.

2015 had been an exceptionally intense year. I was running video productions, directing music videos and producing events for SG50, a year-long nation-wide government initiative to commemorate Singapore's 50 years of independence. Perhaps that was why these panic attacks had gotten so bad. Early into 2016, they were not just showing up at 4:44 a.m. but at any time of the day. I was constantly anxious, even though there was no apparent reason for me to be. This made me frustrated with myself, which catapulted me into feeling anxious that I could not stop being anxious.

I was taken hostage by this state of mind; there was no escaping it. I could not be in a shopping mall and I could not sit still to finish watching a movie. I often felt like punching something to have an outlet for my frustrations. I was afraid of being afraid. Soon I became a prisoner in my own room.

It was difficult to sleep at night. I had to trick my mind to fall asleep 'accidentally'. As I got into bed, my wife, Moy Yin, would intentionally distract me by giving me a back massage or by reading the Bible to me. I could only hope to drift off amid these distractions. The minute I became conscious that I was trying to lie down to sleep, I would jump straight out of bed and walk aimlessly around the house. I had no idea why I kept doing this. Eventually, getting to sleep became a fearful experience. Sometimes, halfway through the bedtime ritual of deceiving myself to sleep, I would laugh over the silliness of it all. It was funny and sad.

To make matters worse, I also lost my sense of smell and taste while fighting a bout of flu during this time. At first I thought it was just the effects of the medication that was making my food tasteless. But soon I realised that I could not smell anything either, which surely had nothing to do with flu medication. Meal times became difficult and frustrating. Even eating wasabi had no effect in kick-starting my senses. I quickly lost my appetite for food.

As our senses are key factors in creating a familiar reality for us, the loss of my ability to smell and taste disorientated me immensely. Space and time became unfamiliar. My bed and workspace did not feel the same anymore. I felt like I was on a different planet and began to question my reality. After about three months of this, I was losing my appetite to live.

Into the Blackest of Black Holes
And then, all of a sudden, out of nowhere, my ears started to ring. I was hit with tinnitus.

As a painter who works with colours, I know there is a kind of black that makes it impossible for light to bounce off of it. It is like the darkness of a black hole that drowns light out completely. This was it, my blackest black, with my incessant panic attacks, no taste and smell, and now a 24/7 ringing sound in my ear so that I can never go to sleep again. I joked with myself (my humour steadily becoming darker too), "So is this how God sounds like? A constant alarm?"

I was shattered. Now I could not even trick myself to sleep because of the loud buzzing in my ears, a sound that no one else could hear. Moy Yin had to drive me around Singapore so that I could try to sleep in the car. The sound and motion of the moving car drowned out the tinnitus and was the only thing that could give me momentary peace.

Albert Camus once said, "The world itself, whose single meaning I do not understand is but a vast irrational. If one could only say just once: 'this is clear', all would be saved".[1] But nothing was clear; this entire situation was absurd. Like Job in the Scriptures, I questioned the meaning of my existence and what I did to deserve this terrible lot in life. In my blackest black, I made a deal with myself: if the ordeal did not improve by the end of the year, I would exit the planet on my own terms.

Searching for Light
Treatment

I went to every doctor who could potentially help me: an ear, nose and throat specialist, a neurologist, a practitioner of Traditional Chinese Medicine, a chiropractor, an Emotional Freedom Techniques therapist and a psychiatrist. I tried every treatment possible: exercise, health supplements, massages, acupuncture, medicine, spiritual counselling and therapy.

Every professional I went to had their own opinion of what was happening to me. They would diagnose me through the lens of their own expertise—the ENT focused on my ear, nose and throat; the chiropractor looked at the balance of my bone structure etc.—and did not assess me as a whole person. The medical doctors were thus only able to be helpful in part. In fact, it was only the TCM doctor who was aware that our bodies need to be seen as a whole (physically, mentally, emotionally etc.). As she treated my physical ailments, she also recommended that I see a psychiatrist. I was finally able to receive the correct

---

1   Albert Camus, *The Myth of Sisyphus and Other Essays*, trans. Justin O'Brien (New York, New York: Vintage Books, 1991), 27.

diagnosis: I had an anxiety disorder. From here, I could start working out a path to recovery.

I am not sure what worked, but my sense of taste slowly returned. I was enraptured every time I tasted something, savouring how wonderful it was to have my senses intact. However, in my anxiety to stay healed, I developed pigeon superstition: "Which supplement healed me? Or was it acupuncture? Or did my prayers finally work?" My mind kept churning out all sorts of theories and I still could not rest.

Prayer
I prayed and cried, and cried and prayed, asking God to make my pain go away divinely. Like a good evangelical, I prayed by quoting Scripture and lamenting like the Psalmists. When that did not stop the panic attacks, I prayed like the Pentecostals by speaking in tongues and claiming God's promises. Then I bargained with Him, as though I had something I could trade with God, for the panic attacks to stop.

I even threatened God by saying His name would be shamed if He did not heal me. After a while, the act of praying became less about having faith in God and more like psychological pain relief. I also reached out to some of my close friends for their prayers. Pastors who heard about what I was going through also encouraged and prayed for me. I was grateful for their support.

Despite this huge 'prayer drive', God stayed silent. Soon, whenever I heard testimonies thanking God for His supernatural healing and intervention, I felt displaced and jealous, like an unwanted child. No matter how much love and attention people poured on me, I still felt like I was drowning. Some kind of acknowledgement from Him would have made me feel better, even if it was as impersonal as an auto-reply email.

While in the midst of this confusing and exhausting darkness, I could not see what God was doing in my life. It was only much later that I realised that God was, in fact, near. It was I who had wandered far away and, in my zeal to be healed, had become 'hard of hearing' by ignoring His still, small voice.

My Wife

Moy Yin is my Wonder Woman. She did things that the movie/comic Wonder Woman would never have been able to do. Besides taking care of the household, she now had a twisted version of a husband to deal with. I know she felt helpless and prayed constantly to God for wisdom. She obeyed the Lord to "keep walking" through this ordeal with me, even though she struggled with having no clarity as to where this road would take us. And God worked miracles through her. During the blackest of times, she was my light. Her face and presence gave me relief and comfort. She was God's answer to my prayers, one that I did not deserve.

I was hit with an exceptionally bad panic attack one evening, the kind that made me want to throw myself off the building. My heart rate was racing. Moy Yin found me crying and moving around the house frantically, begging God to remove the attack. She came to me and started stroking my back. Immediately, I could feel my heart rate slow down drastically. I was pleasantly surprised. It felt like such a miracle! From then on, every time I was hit with another panic attack, I relied on her to stroke my back to calm my internal and physical storm. But this also became a problem, because I started trying to stop her from leaving me alone at home. I became so anxious every time she had to leave for work, terrified that without her I would not be able to stay afloat; I clung to her like a baby.

My Brother-in-Christ

With my constant need for company, and Moy Yin unable to be with me all the time, my loyal and long-suffering brother-in-Christ often came to fill that void. When he came over, it was never with the intention of 'helping' me get out of my situation.

Sometimes, Barnabas just slept on a chair in my office. He trusted me to do what I needed to do to cope, and just wanted to make sure I was safe while I figured things out. Other times, we talked about our shared love for camera gadgets, and church matters. This really took my mind off focusing on myself so much, which was vital to my healing process.

Barnabas' company was a welcome contrast to some people from church who gave well-meaning but unhelpful spiritual advice. They interpreted my situation through spiritual lenses and heaped various healing seminars and camps on my plate. Some became frustrated when I told them I could not attend a retreat because I could not bear to be apart from my wife during that time. One even told me that that was a lie of the devil that stopped me from attending. Sadly, despite their sincerity, their 'help' only reminded me of how alone I was most of the time. It was so precious to have a true brother who was willing to meet me where I was during that period of darkness.

Another brother-in-Christ who had also gone through a mental illness reached out and offered encouragement. It comforted me to know that I was not alone in my struggles. I also kept Barnabas' favourite fragment of Scripture, "And it shall come to pass" (Acts 2:17a, NKJV), close to heart. It gave me hope that everything has a beginning and an end, even this darkest encounter with anxiety disorder. I was grateful that my church's men's ministry had taught us how vital it is to have a brother that we can call at 2 a.m. The few I have were so crucial to my survival.

Breaking Black

Six months later, despite all these efforts, I now could not get out of my room on my own. I passed the time surfing YouTube and stumbled upon a new movie review of the experimental film, *Knight of Cups* by Terrence Malick. I'd always loved the director's works. This particular film of his relied heavily on improvisation—some of the main actors did not even receive a script—and dealt with life's universal existential questions.

I rented the film and watch it. One moment in particular struck me. As the main protagonist, Rick (played by Christian Bale), is in his 'blackest black', a priest tells him,

> *If you are unhappy, you shouldn't take it as a mark of God's disfavor. Just the contrary. Might be the very sign He loves you. He shows His love, not by helping you avoid suffering, by sending you suffering. By keeping you there. To suffer binds you to something higher than yourself. Higher than your own will. Takes you from the world to find what lies beyond it.*

> *We are not only to endure patiently the troubles He sends, we are to regard them as gifts. As gifts more precious than the happiness we wish for ourselves.*[2]

Suddenly, I realised that I had to stop struggling against my situation and fighting to get rid of it in order for true rest to take shape. I had been so afraid of being lost to the meaninglessness of this pain that I was doing my best to go to war with it. But in clinging so tightly to my need to be healed, I was not able to see that this pain was actually a form of God-given rest.

I decided to surrender my pursuit of finding out the reasons for my suffering and channel my strength toward trusting God to take me through it instead. God is light and the blackest black is also light to him (Psalm 139:12, paraphrased). And if hope was not coming to me in the typical 'white and bright' way, in Him, there was a way to see it through the blackest black.

For two weeks, I did nothing but sleep. The medication I received from the psychiatrist also helped put my racing mind to rest. Things started to get better. I had fewer panic attacks. By Christmas I was very much back to myself. It would take one year for me to adjust to the new norm of living with tinnitus and managing stress well. But eventually, I was out of the woods.

This whole experience has awoken me to a new level of consciousness of the divine grace of God. He is the only

---

[2] *Knight of Cups.* Directed by Terrence Malick. (Nashville, Tennessee: Dogwood Films, Los Angeles, California: Waypoint Entertainment, 2015).

one who can see me as a whole person, and knows best what I need. To live a meaningful life, I know that I have to let go of my expectations and rights—even my right to not be in pain—and let Him take the reins. More than ever, He must increase and I decrease. This experience has taken me to the foot of the cross; I am free to begin again.

Mike Wong

NB: Read Mike's son Myer's story on page 78 and his wife Wong Moy Yin's story on page 115.

HOPE IS FINDING BEAUTY IN ASHES

I found it hard to admit that I had fallen into depression, again.

How was I here again, God? A close friend who survived depression told me that there was no way a relapse could happen after my water baptism.

Yet here I was, reliving my darkest nightmare, just four years after my rededication to Christ. Worst of all, the bouts of insomnia and suicidal thoughts were 10 times more consuming than the last experience.

I was in turmoil for fear of judgement and accusations that I was not trying hard enough. Was I really not trusting God enough or not praying enough? Was my faith just not strong enough?

What went wrong, God?

In July 2017, I was 23, a starry-eyed fresh graduate who was eager to take on the world in this next chapter of my life. Everything was going so well for me. But life sent a wrecking ball that shattered my hopes and plans. I went spiralling into an emotional minefield of darkness that would last over a year.

My mum was diagnosed with Ameloblastoma, a rare kind of tumour in the jaw that becomes progressively cancerous if untreated. Hers was caught in the early stages and was miraculously benign. But my family was still in deep distress as we considered the high recurrence rate of this particular cancer, and the long medical and financial battle ahead of us.

Despite being unsettled by my initial anxieties, I committed to surrendering the situation to God. I recognised that the situation was so beyond my control that the best thing I could do was trust that God would look after my mum. While He did that, I decided to help by loving and supporting her through her pain. As the only Christian in the family, I dedicated myself to praying on behalf of my single mum and little sister for a healing miracle. We would get through this together as a family.

At the beginning, I was optimistic and confident in my new role as a caregiver. Recalling how my mum gave her all in bringing up her two daughters single-handedly, I genuinely thought that I was capable of offering her the same love and emotional support during her recovery. I made up my mind to hold off my job-hunting plans to focus on caring for her and co-managing her business once her treatments commenced. However, due to some financial issues and many stressful delays, it was an unexpectedly long wait of five months before the operation took place in late November.

As the weeks went on, I struggled immensely. The five months seemed interminable. I found myself overwhelmed by my mum's frequent emotional outbursts, controlling demands and decision-making. Uncertain about my competency as a caregiver, I wondered whether I was the one who was not being understanding enough. I rationalised that my mum was not herself as she was suffering and did not want to hold her behaviour against her. After all, was it not my duty as her daughter to honour and assure her lovingly? Through this challenging time, I held onto God as best as I could. I prayed that I would be unconditional in my love, believing that if I gave in to and stood by my mum, she would eventually come around.

It's gonna be okay. Everything's gonna be okay after her surgery.

> *I am overwhelmed with troubles and my life draws near to death. I am counted among those who go down to the pit; I am like one without strength ... I am confined and cannot escape; my eyes are dim with grief. (Psalm 88: 3–8)*

The worst was over! Or so I thought. Little did I know that my nightmare would begin after my mum was discharged from the hospital.

The December after her surgery was physically and emotionally exhausting. As her sole caregiver, I persevered in trying to be understanding, patient and loving towards her around the clock for three straight weeks. But by Christmas time, I had fallen into great despair as I felt more and more isolated, unable to find the words to tell someone about what I was going through. Still, I hoped that once I had some rest and resumed my plans, it would all be better in the new year.

Peace was short-lived as my mum dropped a bombshell a few days into the new year. She had decided that I should take another year off work to care for her. She left no room for discussion. My glimmer of hope was shattered. She then began micromanaging everything I did with cutting commands and words. Although she was recovering well, my heart was increasingly crushed as the days went by.

It became suffocating to be at home. I was growing resentful of myself for resenting my mum. All I had done was try to honour her, yet here I was, in so much pain that the colours in my world had begun to fade. This familiar weight of hopelessness that I was feeling again terrified me. It had taken two years for me to overcome depression the first time, would it take just as long this time?

Nothing mattered anymore. It became draining to get out of bed, to breathe, to be functional, to eat, talk or reach out to people. Words started to fail me; I could not even describe what I was feeling. Wracked with guilt and shame, I wept soundlessly into my pillow every night before sleep found me at dawn. Like a haze that formed a seal around my memories, the pain prevented me from recalling God's goodness in my life. All I wanted was for it to stop. I had lost the desire to stay alive.

> *... though I walk through the valley of the shadow of death, I will fear no evil; For You are with me ... (Psalm 23:4, NKJV)*

But right when I had given up, God divinely arranged for me to meet a pastor and a sister-in-Christ. They reminded me that I was still worthy, the apple of God's eye and a conqueror, His precious and beloved daughter, whom He had rescued from the valley of the shadow of death. They exhorted me not to lose hope and told me that I would emerge victorious from this trial.

Through their words, God met me right where I was. All along, I believed that God had forsaken me the moment I dishonoured Him by resenting my mum and causing my own relapse with this bitterness. I replayed these thoughts in my head a million times: all hope was lost; surely no one was coming for me this time because even I detested how far I had fallen. Yet, God did not abandon me. He answered my cries for help by bringing people to speak truth into my heart: He still loved me and I could hope in Him again.

I began to seek help, receiving church counselling while staying accountable to a small and trusted group of church leaders and close friends. I knew from experience that it was too daunting to overcome this on my own. The pain of depression grows more fatal when it stays bottled up in the dark, but would dissipate when exposed to the light. The warm acceptance and encouragement of my little community helped me overcome the fear and shame I felt for relapsing and for burdening them with my problems. They assured me that I was not meant to struggle alone and kept me going through my recovery.

Every week, with every little step I took back to God, He encouraged and assured me that I was doing well. The haze began to lift, and I could now identify the lies of depression and replace it with the truth of God's everlasting promises. It was such a defining moment for me when I learnt that setbacks can happen in anyone's mental health journey. Just like physical illness, mental illness can recur despite one's best efforts to live healthily. It is not something that an individual chooses to have. Rather, it is the result of a complex combination of spiritual, emotional, cognitive and biological issues. And just like physical illness, it cannot simply be willed away without proper treatment. A trite platitude, like "just pray, read your Bible and think positive thoughts," is far from an adequate cure.

It is frustrating and heart-breaking that these misconceptions persist, as they contribute to the stigma that people with mental illness are those who refuse to help themselves. By downplaying or over-spiritualising mental health issues, many who are in legitimate pain are not taken seriously and end up stifled in silence. I was grateful that God brought me people who could dispel my false perceptions about depression; the truth set me free to pursue my recovery with a much lighter heart.

I also learnt that honouring my mum was never supposed to be at the expense of my mental and emotional health. Rather, in order to love others well, I had to love myself first. This truth helped me persevere in setting healthy boundaries between me and my mum, and taking back ownership of my well-being. I decided to take a long overdue grad trip for a month, and then spent another three months serving God by working full time in church on an AlphaTrack programme. During this four-month 'sabbatical', I arranged for my sister to take our mum to her medical appointments so I could focus on building myself back up.

Next, even when I did not feel like it, I confronted the heaviness and lies of depression with praise and proclamations of the goodness of God. I chose to walk in the light and truth of God's Word, intentionally practicing self-care and declaring my assurance in my identity as His beloved child. Despite my mum's initial resistance to my new boundaries, I stuck to them. By God's grace, this healing space and distance was just what we needed to improve our communication channels and restore our relationship. In time, we were able to relate to each other with affection again.

> *Wait for the LORD; be strong and take heart and wait for the LORD. (Psalm 27:14)*

During my recovery, I joined Project Semicolon, a mental health movement that supports those who struggle with mental illness, addiction and thoughts of self-harm and suicide. This project was founded on the concept of the semicolon, the punctuation that signifies the point where someone could have ended a sentence—or his/her own life—but has chosen not to instead.

As a Christian, I believe that I am not the author of my own story. *God is.* In the story He has written for me, trials are commas. They are not meant to be full-stops. And I do not want to put a full-stop where God has not. That decision lies with Him. What I do get to decide is whether I offer my life as a spiritual act of worship (Romans 12:1) even amid my suffering.

Today, I am on the journey of healing and rebuilding my life in the power of God's transformative love. It has been one of praising God and finding beauty in the little progress that I have made towards Him every day. I am learning to love the young woman I see in the mirror: celebrating her, forgiving her, committing to her and being proud of her. I am gradually letting go of my need to be strong, my pursuit of a supposed perfection and my critical self-expectations, so that I do not board every train of thought down towards depression.

There are days when strength looks like nothing more than drawing deep breaths, bravely moving forward from one moment to the next. There are days when it feels like my words, mind and body might fail me. But I know that God never will. He has come through for me in all of my darkest moments in life, and always will. The promise that I am known and loved by God is my greatest treasure. If He had not revealed this truth to me, I would not be alive today. The peace that comes from knowing who I am in Him has given me the courage and purpose to continue living.

Alivia Kan

NOT "TABOO®"

This was the first time we were on holiday as an extended family, my wife and I, our children and their fiancés. It was just six weeks before our only daughter was to be married and a couple of days since I'd started on Lexapro® (Escitalopram) for depression. As I tried to play Taboo with the people I loved most, I wasn't sure if it was the medication or the depression that was causing me to be in quite a state. I felt moody and lousy; I couldn't concentrate, focus or think quickly. It was awful. Taboo was a game I had enjoyed countless times before with my family. And I'd done well at it too! But here I was, struggling to concentrate, losing both the game and my sanity, and forcing myself to laugh and appear happy even though I was crying inside.

Rock Bottom

The last year or so before the "Taboo®" episode had been rough. It wasn't just the amount of work that I'd been saddled with that drove me to depression. Rather, it was a constant stream of challenging relational issues that affected me the most. Being questioned by both my leaders and my patients about the recommendations I'd made in the latter's best interests slowly generated negativism in my spirit. Allowing passive anger to build up against a colleague instead of lovingly confronting him made me feel even more irritable and upset. I am not a naturally confrontational person, and the thought of needing to do it—even though I knew it was the right thing to do—brought me great emotional distress.

To top it all off, I was struggling hard to cope with "losing" my precious daughter once she got married. Archibald D. Hart's words in his book *Unmasking Male Depression* summed this feeling up well,

> *Then there was the time when my first daughter was going to be married. I found myself quite depressed a few months before the wedding. Finally, it dawned on me that my little girl was saying good-bye to me in favor of a young man who was not part of me. Like it or not, being excited for my daughter was not enough to overcome my sense of sadness. I was facing a loss that could never be replaced. There were those who said to me, "You're not losing a daughter but gaining a son-in-law." What a ridiculous idea! What I was losing could not be counterbalanced by what I was gaining. Every father of a daughter knows that a son-in-law does not equal a daughter!*[1]

Coming across that passage was like hitting the jackpot. Finally, I felt understood.

The combination of all these difficulties led me to feeling upset, tired, irritable and angry almost daily. I teared easily. Incessant negative, even suicidal, thoughts occupied my mind. I couldn't sleep well even though I was so tired most days. I kept waking up at 4 a.m., which added to

---

1   Archibald D. Hart. *Unmasking Male Depression: Recognizing the Root Cause to Many Problem Behaviors, Such as Anger, Resentment, Abusiveness, Silence, Addictions, and Sexual Compulsions* (Nashville, Tennessee: Thomas Nelson, 2001), 128.

my frustration, hopelessness, guilt, sense of worthlessness and exhaustion. After being in denial for a while, and hoping that my spirits would lift with time, rest and exercise, the inevitable truth that I was in clinical depression started to sink in. Things were only becoming worse as the low moods and negative thoughts intensified persistently.

Seeking Help
I resisted seeking help early as I was a medical practitioner and worried that patients may not want to consult a doctor with depression. But I realised that carrying on without seeking help was unfair to the ones I loved. I had reached a point where nothing really mattered anyway, and did not care about the stigma associated with taking anti-depressants. I plucked up the courage to see a psychiatrist and started on medication.

I really should not have been concerned about the fact that I was a doctor with depression. Given the stressful nature of this vocation—one that is not only technically demanding but also emotionally taxing—depression among doctors is far more common than is publicly known. A news article in January 2019 reported that, according to a survey conducted by Medscape, close to 44 percent of US physicians are burnt out, and 15 percent are depressed and think about suicide. Furthermore, the report revealed that more than one doctor per day commits suicide—a rate higher than any other profession and more than twice that of the general population.[2] These shocking statistics have helped me recognise how important it is not to

---

2   "No Quick Fix for Physician Burnout, Depression." *CNA*, January 16, 2019. Accessed June 19, 2019. https://www.channelnewsasia.com/news/health/no-quick-fix-for-physician-burnout--depression-11131580.

belittle the stress that I was feeling from work and to ask for help before it is too late.

Finding Normality
Even though I did not suffer too many side effects from Escitalopram, the first week of taking them (during that holiday with my family where I was trying to play Taboo) made me feel worse. But things started to improve after a few weeks. Although I was still feeling low a month later, I was far less weepy. (In fact, I was rather "numb". At a colleague's funeral, many men were sobbing away while I was strangely dry-eyed and emotionless.)

But about three and half months after starting the medication, I was definitely feeling and functioning much better. I had no more suicidal thoughts and the lingering negative ones were far less intense than usual. My feelings of hopelessness were also mostly gone. But I was not yet "walking on clouds", so my psychiatrist and I decided to increase the dosage of my medication. A week later, I distinctly remember waking up one morning and thinking, "Oh, is this what it feels like to be normal?" That morning, after many, many months of feeling down, moody and negative, I finally felt happy and was looking forward to the day's work.

It has been more than four years since I started on Escitalopram in December 2014. I have tried weaning off medication and could, at one stage, go off it for a few months. However, I function much better with them and have no qualms about remaining on them long-term. A model I came across from the Canadian Mental Health Association[3] was very helpful in giving me a paradigm shift.

Two-continuum Model

Essentially, it emphasises that people who are taking medication for a mental health condition can actually be psychologically and emotionally healthier than (a) people who *do not* have a diagnosed mental health condition, or (b) people who *do* have a mental health condition but have chosen not to take medication. In other words, medication is not an indication of one's weakness. It is merely a means that enables one to live freely. As a physician, I resonated with this concept, as I often say something similar about diabetic or hypertensive patients: patients who take medication for their high blood sugar levels or

---

3 "Mental Health Information." *CMHA Ontario*. Accessed June 19, 2019. http://ontario.cmha.ca/documents/positive-mental-health-and-well-being/.

blood pressure will be in better health than people who have these conditions but refuse their medication. Their medication keeps their sugar levels and blood pressure in control while those who refuse medication are at much greater risk of health complications. Likewise, a patient who has a mental health condition but refuses to go on medication is likely to suffer ill effects and poor daily functioning compared to one who takes medication to keep symptoms at bay.

Apart from medication, I have also learnt to rely on the grace that God provides to sustain me. Christopher Ash reminds me not to pay "lip-service" to grace:

> *Despite being a dedicated gospel-hearted Christian who preached grace, the truth is that I was dangerously close to living a gospel of works, not grace.*[4]

Many born-again Christians claim to live under grace but the way we conduct our affairs, and our impatience with ourselves and others, seem to indicate otherwise. This tendency to strive often leads to overwork and is the recipe for burnout and depression. In contrast, one of the key ways that God gives us grace is through His provision of rest. Instead of working myself to exhaustion, I now take regular breaks to maintain my mental health. Although there have also been many times when I wished I could do more, without regular rest, I know I will not be productive in helping others. W. Phillip Keller says it well, "The surprising truth is that the person who pauses long enough

---

4 Christopher Ash, *Zeal without Burnout* (New Malden, London: The Good Book Company, 2016), 43.

to refresh his soul along the way actually becomes more alert, more alive, more efficient."[5] As a Christian, observing the weekly Sabbath intentionally as a time of rest from work and worship has also been fundamental. I remember that, "God needs no day off. But I am not God, and I do."[6] The Sabbath reminds me that it is God who gives me strength, so that even in unpredictable and unwanted events, I can rest in the thought echoed by the psalmist:

> *The lines have fallen for me in pleasant places; indeed, I have a beautiful inheritance. (Psalm 16:6, ESV)*

The imagery is so wonderful in this verse. I imagine a picture of chaotic lines that the Lord Jesus miraculously arranges into a neat order. It gives me hope for what He will do with my life. No matter how chaotic or negative it may seem to be at some points, I know that in the end, everything will fall nicely into place because God has promised me a beautiful inheritance. This hope makes the physical and emotional imperfections that I have to live with on earth so much easier to bear.

Overcoming Stigma

Contrary to what I had expected; family, patients and friends were absolutely supportive and encouraging when I decided to be open about what I was going through. Support from those who care is so essential in the road to recovery.

---

5 W. Phillip Keller, *Strength of Soul* (Grand Rapids, Michigan: Kregel, 1993), 26.
6 Ash, *Zeal*, 61.

At the end of the family holiday after my horrible performance at Taboo®, I decided to open up to my two adult children and their fiancés. I am thankful that they took it very well and were very encouraging. My wife, who knew of my struggles all along, had been a pillar of strength when my world was crumbling emotionally. She is my best confidante, my best friend, makes me laugh, reminds me to rest and is ever patient with me when I'm negative and moody. Best of all, she scratches my back to help me sleep! God must be the One who gives her the strength and grace to put up with me.

I have since grown in being able to accept that I have depression. On top of my family's support, going through several online Cognitive Behavioural Therapy (CBT) modules, as well as reading the Bible and other Christian literature on depression and burn out, have helped immensely. I have discovered that many biblical and historical spiritual giants—both past and present—struggled with depression. They include David, Elijah, Jeremiah, Charles Spurgeon, Henri Nouwen, Martin Luther and John Piper. Knowing that it was all right to be Christian and depressed has been very helpful.

One of my favourite verses comes from Psalm 18:

> *For it is you who light my lamp; the LORD my God lightens my darkness. For by you I can run against a troop, and by my God I can leap over a wall. This God—his way is perfect; the word of the LORD proves true; he is a shield for all those who take refuge in him. (Psalm 18:28–30, ESV)*

In my moments of darkness and depression, I am comforted by the fact that it is God who will ultimately light my darkness. While medication, therapy and support are all valuable; they do not heal me completely on their own. At the end of the day, God is the Only One who can bring healing. As someone who had problems scaling a low wall in the obstacle course during my time in the army, the imagery of God empowering me to the extent of running against a troop and leaping over a wall is especially encouraging.

I would be lying if I said that I am totally comfortable with being transparent about my depression in all circumstances. There are still many occasions when I feel uneasy, especially amongst acquaintances. When disclosing the fact for the first time in a group, there is always that thought, no matter how tiny, that the news might not be well received. Thankfully though, this has not happened.

The stigma associated with mental illness is still very real in Singapore and other countries in Asia. That is why I have chosen to be open about my own situation. Many employers do not understand that mental health patients well controlled on medication can function as well, if not better than "normal" people. This is probably why many people fear disclosing their condition at the workplace.

It is my prayer that with increased awareness, employers will be open to accepting applicants with a history of mental illness but who are stable on medication. As long as a person is capable of performing the job and does not pose a danger to himself/herself or others, he/she should be given equal opportunities. It is my hope that society as a whole will seek to understand mental illness better so that they will be more understanding, supportive and even helpful to those who are struggling with it.

Dr George Khoo

Dr George Khoo is a family physician in his late 50s. George is married to Mabel and they have two adult children, both happily married. George and Mabel enjoy their time as grandparents to four lovely girls.

CHASING ANGELS, CHASING ETERNITY

It began in 2015. My uncle told me he was calling the ambulance because my grandmother's helper told him that I was acting weirdly at night. Scared, I packed a few belongings and rushed out of the house before the ambulance could arrive to take me away. I went to the nearest Coffee Bean and sat there thinking about what I should do. I decided to book a room in a backpackers' hostel, which I ended up staying in for about four months. Subsequently, one day in a restaurant, I thought a person was squirting strange substances at me and reacted by throwing plates and dishes at him. The police came to the restaurant and took me to the Institute of Mental Health (IMH). It turned out that what I thought the man was doing did not actually happen.

At IMH, I was diagnosed with schizophrenia. A while later, I also started having psychosis. I imagined that my father, who had committed suicide when I was two years old, was alive. I was subsequently asked to leave my job.

It was challenging trying to overcome the hallucinations of my father, keeping a job, and paying for my expenses all at the same time. But I received a lot of support from my church friends in Cornerstone Community Church. They visited me in IMH whenever I was warded and bought muffins and potato chips, much to my delight. They prayed for me in the ward and reminded me that God's peace, which transcends all understanding, was bestowed on me. They also helped me whenever I needed to shift to a new rental room. This was very important to me, as I feel very distressed every time I move to a new place and have to deal with a new landlord. One of my cell members also owns a dog called Mike. Mike helps in my recovery. When I visit that cell member's house, I can play with Mike. He is ever so gentle when he responds to me each time I call his name.

My cell-group leader consistently reminds me that I am in her prayers. This gives me strength as I believe prayers form a protective shield around me wherever I go. Every time I quit a job, I tell my cell-group leader. She advises me to pray over it, listen to worship songs and meditate upon God's Word. It helps that someone knows about what I am going through and that I am not alone in this.

Yet, as my Christian friends are high-functioning working adults, they may not always understand my day-to-day struggles or the depth of the fears I have about life. Having stability is greatly lacking in the life of someone recovering from mental illness. I have quit jobs on my second day at work, taken three months to find another one, only to quit again after two days, because I never quite know the effects that new medication will have on me.

Sometimes, the medication makes me sleepy in the daytime so it is difficult to wake up for work. At the invisible hands of my anti-psychotic pills, I have even fallen asleep at my workplace before. When my supervisor confronted me about this, I felt guilty for doing something wrong. Since work is an act of worship, I also wondered if God was displeased with me for falling asleep in the middle of work. I was determined not to eat the medicine so that I would not let God down again. Fortunately, my psychiatrist listened to my fears and changed my medication to an injection instead, which does not cause sleepiness or drowsiness.

Another type of medicine made my legs shake so furiously that I could not sit still for long. I had to take a muscle relaxant to counteract this side-effect. I would pop one before work and another near the end of the work day. On days that I forget to bring the second pill, I would have to rush home to eat the second pill to stop my legs from going out of control. When the medicine keeps me from doing my job in a comfortable manner, I am reminded that my mental illness cripples me from living a normal life. It makes me feel resigned at times that I have to suffer in silence and bear the side effects of the medicine that is managing my mental condition. I remember praying furiously and silently to God once, when the muscle relaxant wore off right in the middle of a church sermon. I started stamping my feet vigorously and a church friend asked if I could be quieter because the loud noise was distracting the others in the auditorium. I felt so helpless and could only trust that God would miraculously calm my twitching muscles to give me rest.

It is also very difficult when the devil puts the thought that I am useless in my mind. Once, in 2018, I believed this so much that I actually attempted suicide. I warded myself in IMH and took 129 pills that I had previously been given for my psychosis. I woke up in Sengkang General Hospital, where I was sent after I was found unconscious. This loneliness is something my Christian community might not understand, for they think that if I pray and read the Bible, God will surely supply all my needs and I would not be tempted to overdose. But not having a stable job makes it challenging to pay rent, as I have to rely on my savings, which can run out. The anxiety that I feel each time while waiting for a new job to come cannot be underestimated. But even though my church friends may not always have been there to support me through all my fears, I know they do care. When I WhatsApp them, I usually get replies on the same day.

I now have a case manager from IMH whom I can speak to whenever I am suicidal and have anxiety attacks. She goes with me to my IMH appointments and ensures that I get my medications on time. She has helped me set up a personal safety plan, which has been tremendously helpful. I have set tasks that I can embark on whenever I feel suicidal, such as listening to worship songs, watching YouTube and Netflix, calling SOS, messaging my church cellmates, or cooking instant noodles. Making a simple meal gives me a sense of achievement and determination, as it reminds me of how much I want to have a place of my own. I place this personal safety plan in a prominent place above my bed, where I can see it every night before I go to sleep.

Right now, I am in my recovery journey where I do not have to take oral medications but only need monthly injections for schizophrenia. Although I was in and out of IMH and was hospitalised four times in 2018, I have not been warded in 2019. I have been in the Early Psychosis Intervention Programme for the past three years, as it is for people who are in the first three years of diagnosis. I have also attended a three-day peer support class that prepares me to be a peer support specialist, if I decide to sign up for the National Council of Social Service course.

I can see God's hand in my journey by how He has provided for me. Despite the difficulties I have had with keeping a job, God has provided part-time work for me, like flyer distribution and telemarketing, so that I can earn some money. I feel His hand over my life as I listen to worship songs. It reminds me that His peace that transcends all understanding will guide my mind and heart, and I can sing even in the middle of a storm. I feel God's hand in my recovery even as I go through counselling sessions with my case manager. Through these sessions, I have learnt about how my thoughts become actions, so I need to manage what I think about, and how important it is to spend my time meaningfully.

My hope is in God's love during this season. Although some days I struggle to believe it, deep down I know He loves me despite my imperfections. I pray that I will not have psychoses or hallucinations again so that I can keep a good job, and have money for my rent, living expenses, and savings for a rainy day. God's love will heal my brokenness. This is the hope that I hold on to.

Dayne Hor

WALKING IN THE PATH OF LIFE

I first met Wong Hui Chew on the streets of Holland Village. He was just a wheelchair-bound, tissue paper seller uncle to me then. But after he befriended me, I learnt that he had many struggles in his life. He is stateless, formerly homeless, diagnosed with Anxiety State (among other physical illnesses), and suffers from confusion and memory loss. Yet, none of these labels have ever defined him. I discovered that Hui Chew knew that his true identity was in being a beloved child of God, and Abba Father has never forgotten him.

Here is Hui Chew's story.

Locked In
It happened at 6 a.m. I remember the smell of the early morning rain.

They found Mama and me sleeping at Tanjong Pagar MRT (Mass Rapid Transit) station; huddled, bleary-eyed and confused, as the voices of the MCYS (Ministry of Community Development, Youth and Sports) officers pierced our uneasy slumber.

I knew we were in trouble because Mama had no identity card, and my nationality indicates 'UNKNOWN', because I was born as a stateless almost-Singaporean. We also had strained relationships with our family members, so there was nowhere for us to go. The officers had no choice but to put us in the place designated for people who do not belong anywhere: the Home for the Destitute, located next to IMH (Institute of Mental Health) or Woodbridge Hospital, as it was known at that time.

They separated Mama and me, placing us in rooms and sections according to our gender. My room had windows with metal grilles. I felt trapped, alone and scared.

Later that morning, I asked the male staff on duty how I could leave this place. Used to dealing with people in my situation on a daily basis, he replied indifferently and said that we could only leave if a family member came to bring us home. I felt a strong sense of hopelessness; I knew no one was going to come.

Compared to a prisoner, who knows his/her period of sentencing, my confinement was so indefinite, so uncertain, and so much at the mercy of others. Was I going to be locked inside until the day I stopped breathing? The thought that even my corpse would remain in this place and never have the chance to leave was paralysing.

I was so traumatised by the whole experience that I could not eat anything that afternoon. One of the staff members noticed this and said, "Don't think that by refusing to eat, we will allow you to leave." Upon hearing this, I became even more nervous. I asked him how long was I going to have to stay in this place? And for the second time that day, I heard, "If your family members don't come for you, we will put you up in a shelter. We will send your mother to an old folks home." It terrified me. They were as good as telling me that I would have no more freedom.

Once I was forced into a shelter, and separated from my mother against my will, I would no longer have a chance to make my own decisions about my life. My mother was quite old at that time; I did not know how much longer I had left to spend with her. What gave them the right to separate us? I could not understand how these people could enforce their will on us and make such a heartless decision like this. Did our rights not count for anything?

As my thoughts started to run wild, I asked to see my doctor at IMH. I could feel my hands and feet heating up, and my body felt like it was floating, signs that I was experiencing an anxiety attack, a condition that I had been diagnosed with since I was 28 years old. I knew that if I just had the chance to speak to my doctor, he would find a way to save me. However, the staff completely ignored my request, cutting off all hope I had of leaving the place, and regaining my freedom and dignity. I had no more options. At 5 p.m. that afternoon, I could not bear the fear and hopelessness anymore. I attempted suicide in the Home by drinking bleach.

The staff called an ambulance and I was admitted into Changi Hospital. The doctor sent me for an X-ray after giving me some medication, and the scan indicated that my stomach was damaged. They arranged for a surgery at dawn. Before the surgery, I remember seeing some nurses praying for me, even though I know hospital staff are usually not supposed to do that. It was so encouraging to me at that point. At my wits' end, emptied of any hope and internal strength to carry on, knowing that even one person cared enough to pray for me was such a source of strength and motivation.

The doctors told me that if I had arrived 30 minutes later, I would not be here today. Surely, it was God who saved my life that day.

Struck Down

Three days later, the hospital transferred me to IMH. The staff contacted our family friend and sister-in-Christ, Bee Keow. She agreed to sign the papers that would allow my mother and me to leave IMH to live with her. Even though it was inconvenient for her and her family to take us in as they live in a small rental flat, she was still willing to make this sacrifice. Because of Bee Keow, I did not end up living in the Home forever.

During my stay with Bee Keow, I tried to find employment. Getting a job is a challenge for me not only because of my citizenship status, but also because I am illiterate. When I was young, my mother had to work very hard to support our family. She had two jobs, one in the morning and the other at night, and would scrape together about $400 a month. However, instead of using the money to send me to school, my father spent it on drinking and gambling. I lost my chance to study. (And as my father was often physically aggressive towards her, my mother eventually decided to leave the house and took me along with her to stay on the streets.) Being illiterate keeps me from doing simple things, like reading road signs and filling out job application forms. But despite all these obstacles, I persevered. As long as I was physically able, I wanted to be responsible for my own life and not place the burden of supporting us financially on my elderly mother. I eventually managed to find some work selling used clothes for a period of time.

I felt very grateful to Bee Keow for saving Mama and me from the Home and wanted to be helpful to her family. One day, I rode my bicycle to Ghim Moh Market and Food Centre to buy duck rice for her son. At the hawker centre, I slipped on the wet floor in the public toilet. When I fell, my lower spine hurt very badly. But I chose to ignore the pain, partially because I did not want to be admitted into another institution after my experience at the Home for the Destitute. After enduring it for a few months, the pain subsided. However, that was when my legs started feeling much weaker. Within a short span of three months, I could no longer walk.

I felt so much regret then. *Why did I not go to the hospital? Why did I buy food for her son?* I was stuck inside the house for almost six months, feeling depressed and very low. It was at this point that I first heard the Mandarin worship song *Chu Ni Yi Wai* (Besides You), which describes how God is the strength of our heart, and how we have no one else beside Him here on earth. The lyrics kept me from being overwhelmed with despair. They made me feel hope that, with Him, something good could still come out of my life.

As I am stateless, I am not eligible for hospital subsidies. I cannot even have a CHAS (Community Health Assist Scheme) card. But when I went for my appointment with the diabetes doctor at NUH, I found out that they were able to give me special subsidies. My doctor arranged for me to visit the orthopaedic doctor in two weeks. But since I could not read the appointment card, I missed my slot. They rescheduled me for the next available slot, which was only six months later. I was relieved that I did not have to go to the hospital then. I was afraid that I would get lost trying to get there because I could not read the road signs, and I was terrified of being trapped in a room by myself again. As a result of this entire incident, I have permanently lost my ability to walk.

But for the Grace of God
Yet, even though my negligence caused my health to deteriorate, I praise God because He still preserved me. I have maintained good use of my arms and upper body, and am not confined to a bed for life. God also sent me help through a church sister, Sun Xiao Jian. She, and other church members, paid for my medical bills and bought me an electric wheelchair. Some Christian brothers and sisters now also accompany me to my hospital appointments, especially since I am scared to go alone.

Living with anxiety is not easy. Sometimes it kicks in whenever I see metal grilles or items that remind me of bad experiences I had when I was younger. I become overwhelmed and am unable to think clearly. Other times, when I see homeless people, I feel scared that I may have to someday go back to a life where I have no home, no shelter, and no family. I try not to be too distressed by these thoughts, and turn my anxiety into motivation to continue with my work instead. I know I need to work hard in order to have money, so at least I can have a roof over my head.

Since I became a Christian, God has sent many brothers and sisters to care for me. In my anxious moments, they answer my phone calls and pray for me. I am always surprised when they pick up the phone, as I know it is not easy for them to talk to me whenever I am upset. But talking to them lightens my burdens and fears; I always feel much better afterwards.

In 2011, Mama got very sick with diabetes and kidney failure. She had to be warded for six months. I knew that she would go to heaven when she passed on because she had accepted Jesus as her God in 2010, but I still felt very sad at the thought of losing her. Throughout my life, whether we lived at home, on the streets, or in Bee Keow's flat, she had always been by my side. Even though she did not understand what anxiety was, she would tell me not to feel bad and encourage me to spend more time with my friends. She was where I felt at home.

But during this difficult time, God brought many brothers and sisters from church to help me. One brother gave me $250 a month, and offered me help whenever I asked for it. Bee Keow made my daily meals for me, as I was only earning less than $10 a day from picking up cardboard and recycling them. And on the day of Mama's funeral, many people from church came to mourn with me. They set up the funeral at the void deck and organised the collection of *bai jin* (literally, white gold; practically, donations for the funeral expenses). Their love consoled me and made me feel like I was one of them.

What my Christian family has done for me is something that money cannot buy. Even though I have lost Mama, I now feel like I have been given a new family. I hope that I will get to meet more brothers and sisters in Christ, because the love of God's family is something precious that I cherish very much.

In the process of writing my story, a Christian sister brought me to take photographs to document the significant places in my life. As I saw the Destitute Home from the outside and recalled the memories, fear took over my body and my hands started to tremble. The only thought that kept running through my mind was to commit suicide once again.

It was at this point that I felt God tell me, "Come, give me your hand". I was suddenly aware of how much Abba Father dotes on and loves me. As someone who has faced rejection many times in life, receiving God's unconditional love is something indescribable. If this sovereign and almighty God was holding my hand, I knew I was going to be safe with Him. That day, I felt so assured that He would help me overcome my old fears, and that I would be able to face any new obstacles together with Him and the family of Christ.

Just as God has sent many people to help me during the various seasons of my life, my greatest hope is to become someone who can help others as well. I want to tell those who have struggles like mine that God can help us and give us strength to carry on. I also hope that just as God has helped me walk in freedom spiritually, He will also help me walk in freedom physically and mentally one day.

Hui Chew

NB: Hui Chew's story was ghostwritten by Anne*.

FINDING GOD IN THE DARK

Dropping into Darkness
As I crossed the road that was winding into the hospital, I didn't check for traffic. I no longer cared about anything at that point. I couldn't feel anything except for the huge weight in my heart. I just wanted it all to end.

On the surface, I am not a likely candidate for depression. I am happily married, and have two boys who bring a lot of laughter to the household. I have attended the same church for more than 10 years, and I believe in salvation through faith in Christ Jesus. I had also recently started a new job that was challenging, meaningful and fun.

Yet, just when I finally started to find new meaning in what I did from 9 a.m. to 5 p.m., I found myself plagued with intense suicidal thoughts. It also became difficult to control my emotions: I either lashed out and raged whenever I felt despondent and hopeless, or felt that my tears were choked up in a ball behind my throat and could not come out.

There had been no obvious trigger to cause the change. Although the doctors would eventually diagnose me with dysthymia, nothing could really explain why I sunk so fast into this major episode of depression. I suspect that after years of ploughing through and trying to make sense of why I was working, this was the first time I was finally starting to enjoy my work. And with that sense of joy, my worn-out brain felt like it no longer had to guard against the frequent toxic thoughts that came when life was not so easy going. For reasons that I still cannot quite explain to myself, without this defence mechanism, I mentally collapsed at the slightest hint of stress.

With the help of my doctor and the support of my supervisors, I took a break to try to heal. But even the beauty of parks and nature, or the peace of a cat cafe, were not enough to help me feel better. I continued to try to reach God to seek His help and healing. I prayed until I reached the darkest place within myself and had no strength to go any further. In the midst of the darkest darkness, even my hope in prayer was extinguished. I could not think straight anymore.

Caught in that downward spiral, I almost started to implement my final plan. Suicide at that point was not simply an escape from the pain, I sincerely felt that it would be better for everyone if I disappeared from this world. But God's grace intervened, prompting me to make one last call to the Mental Health Helpline of a public hospital in Singapore. Someone picked up on the other end, and talked me into taking a bus to the hospital emergency room. On the way, I sent a message to my Bible study group. My wife had to take care of the children and could not go with me.

God guided my steps. As I shambled and plodded across that road into the emergency room, too despondent to care, too tired to cry, He was with me. He had two of my Bible study group members rush down to join me until I was admitted to the hospital for my own safety. He had me transferred to a ward more conducive to my recovery after one night in an acute ward with patients suffering from various forms of mental illnesses. He brought many to visit me in my time of need, and I felt peace and comfort for the first time in a very long time. Many tears were shed. Many words were spoken, written, both to God and from God, through my pastor, through my Bible study mates, through my wife, in my notebook, in a heartfelt letter to my wife.

It's been a year and a half since I admitted myself into the hospital and I still struggle with recovery. I do not know when or where the journey will end. I cannot work because even the slightest stress causes me to lose control of my emotions and overreact. I can spend a full day not wanting to talk, because I just cannot even summon the energy to use more than monosyllables.

But where is God in my life?

Walking Without Anxiety
Many depression sufferers and depressives struggle with anxiety disorder as well, in significant numbers. I am one of the exceptions, by God's grace.

When the depression first hit, I kept asking God for healing if He was willing. As it became evident that He wasn't, it did hit me hard as I felt that I wasn't being heard. But as I prayed in the safety of the hospital, I remember hearing His clear voice letting me know that He was with me. He has never answered my question on how long recovery will take, except through hints from my therapist and my wife that it will take longer than I keep thinking it will. He has also not seen fit to let me know His ultimate purpose for my suffering. Yet I no longer ask God to heal me as often as I used to. I recognise that through this journey with depression, I am developing patience and learning to entrust things that are not within my control into His hands.

The beginning of learning to trust happened during the second night of my hospital stay. As the fog started to lift for the first time, I worried about how my kids would react, how my work would turn out, and whether I was going to lose my job. But God prompted me to let Him take care of those things, for I had a journey ahead of me to undertake. I cried a little then, moved by His kindness. I thank God that by His grace, even though the fog still descends from time to time (though, thankfully, never to that intensity that led me towards disaster), I have still been able to trust Him to handle those worries.

On some things, though, this condition prevents me from being able to function normally. At the best of times, I can take no words of praise or comfort from others. But most days, I simply hate myself with a passion. No amount of reminders that God loves me has managed to shift that hatred a hair. With therapy though, I have identified some of the root issues that have led me to think so hatefully about myself and can now understand why I cannot yet wrench myself out of it. God has graced me with a very effective and caring therapist who is patient and yet firm, as needed, when needed. With her care and guidance, I am starting on the next step of my journey: to learn to love myself just a little bit more.

Considering the depths of what I'm struggling with, not being anxious is an amazing gift. Those with anxiety alongside their depression suffer even more than I do.

They are mentally and physically unable to control their anxiety because of their disorder, and struggle even more with guilt from not being able to overcome two forms of mental illness. I do feel for them, and believe they deserve to be understood and regarded with compassion. (I am certainly not saying that my faith is stronger than those who struggle with anxiety. God simply has His reasons for allowing us to struggle with different things.) Perhaps it is this thankfulness in being spared from it that gives me clarity to focus on doing what He sets before me: my recovery and helping others through their mental and emotional pain.

Walking With Gratitude

God has blessed our family with my steadfast and amazingly faithful wife. She is faithful to God, to our marriage, and to our children. As she grappled with the knowledge that I had almost ended my life, she prayed and left the worst of the situation to God. Meanwhile, she attended to the tasks that were within her control, such as taking care of the boys, making sure the house was kept in good condition, and working on her home baking. With God's grace empowering her to create stability for our family, I knew I could rely on her when I returned home and tried to pick up the pieces of my shattered mind.

In the midst of the pain, I found the ability to express myself through words. In an amazing 'coincidence' that only the Spirit can orchestrate, the digital tablet I had bought for work became my platform to push out comics about depression. And for this, I give thanks. Even when I cannot speak because I have social withdrawal, those words can continue to go on to make an impact in the lives of others. Our church and my extended family have been supporting us financially. My wife, my sons and I are able to eat and afford most things we need. Every time a bill comes in, I give thanks for a loving church and a loving family and a loving Father. We can even afford a bit of luxury at times, because of the little earnings that my wife brings in from her home baking. The baking is her outlet for creativity even as it earns us a little extra. If I had any joy to express, I would say her creations are a joy to behold.

The boys are doing well enough in school. I am grateful that I can spend time around them, even if I cannot be present to them. With the little they know about my condition, they are very supportive of me.

I still struggle with depression, but how can I not thank God? How can I not help but see His hand in my life, guiding, protecting, shepherding me? When I can pray now, I pray. When I can concentrate to read His Word now, I read. I still remember that dark period where I couldn't even pray because everything was so painful and it took all my energy to focus on staying alive. Concentration still does not come easily to me, so being able to read His Word is an amazing honour and gift.

Sufferers of depression are often told to be thankful, as though having gratitude and a 'change of perspective' will suddenly snap us out of being depressed. It doesn't. But it is not to say that a posture of gratitude has no role in my life. As I give thanks for the many things God has provided, I am reminded that He has not abandoned me in my suffering for a minute. The painful path that I must take is still before me, but I am conscious now that He is there every foot of the way. God the Father, Christ His Son, and the Holy Spirit will see me—and my family—through.

Someone asked me once, "Do you regret having depression?" My answer remains the same. It is painful beyond imagination. The tears, the pain, the breathing difficulties, the curling up in a ball to fend off the arrows of the mind; none of these things are enjoyable. Yet after all that I've learnt about myself through my writing and drawing my comics, after all that I've had the privilege to witness as I have helped others in similar pain, and after sharing in their suffering…

I don't regret having depression one bit. And I'm thankful that God has never ever left me alone in the pain.

Walking to Share and Love

While in the ward, I was prompted by the Spirit to prepare to tell my story with two aims in mind. The first was to bring more awareness to what depression looked like from the inside. I had never felt this bad, even during an earlier bout of depression in 2006, and I wanted to let others know that this was a condition that could be helped.

There have been many opportunities for me to speak about my experience with depression. I spend time with fellow sufferers to let them know that they are not alone. I volunteer to speak to school students who visit the public hospital where I had been admitted, to let them know that depression is real and has a face. I have also been given other speaking engagements. Even though social situations tend to leave me mute, by God's grace, I have been able to speak well enough to these assemblies. How else can I do this, if not by His enabling and the strength imparted by the Spirit? The second was to let others know that even Christians can suffer from mental illness. This did not mean that they were weaker than others just because they were affected by such an affliction. And it certainly should not call their salvation into question.

Along the way, I have met Christians who try to suggest practical options that they insist will help with my depression, like aromatherapy or eating certain foods or wearing certain clothes. Medically these 'solutions' are unproven, and only lift the spirits for short moments without doing much to heal depression in the long run. I have also met Christians who seem to think that I lack certain elements of faith, such as thankfulness, or a belief that God will heal me. Others have even questioned whether I was really saved if I have mental illness.

It has been heart-breaking to receive these comments. They have only loaded me with more guilt and confusion, rather than helping me overcome depression. After all, if my mind is already broken and needs to heal, how will burdening me with doubts about the strength of my faith be of any help? How is it loving? If one suggests to someone already pierced with many unseen wounds in his heart and brain that he is not saved, when his faith may be the last thing he is clinging onto for hope, it can be the last straw to destroy him.

Comfort, however, is never wrong. There is always a place for words of care, support, encouragement, reminders of God's love and of what the sufferer means to his loved ones. Gently, with words of love, walk with them back into the light. Caregivers do not need to assume the responsibility of bringing healing to a sufferer; even therapists say that they are only guides to recovery. Ultimately, recovery is still up to the individual sufferer, learning new methods of thought processing, keeping up with their

God-granted medications, and so on. And when it comes to guiding a sufferer out of the maze of pain, nothing can top the grace of God.

Who can grasp His infinite wisdom? Who can fathom the depths of His love? Even though I know I am loved, the belittling nature of this condition makes it easy to feel that I am not worthy of His love. Yet He always holds out a ray of hope, or a word of love, through the people around me and the situations He places me in. This helps me give thanks constantly and recognise that the Lord has a plan for me. I know that I just need to keep fighting, even on days that depression knocks me so low that I am all but crawling. With His help and His care, I now know that even standing still is alright. The comfort I derive from this knowledge is immense. Even if I cannot forgive myself, God has.

One day I might beat the beast. I do not know what job I will do in the future. But I am not worrying about it. I will just try to keep walking in trust into the deep unknown.

God wants me to stay alive.

Mak Kean Loong

WHEN DEPRESSION DROVE ME AWAY FROM GOD

I sank to the floor of the toilet and sobbed uncontrollably. I'd tried everything: I'd taken my antidepressants and was already on the *third* type of medicine that my psychiatrist prescribed me; I'd seen my psychologist regularly and was trying to develop a less sedentary life; I'd tried to believe people when they told me they cared about me. And yet, my heart was still stricken with pain and my soul was wracked with brokenness every moment of the day.

The thing about depression is that after you seek treatment, the lows come and go at really unexpected moments. It comes suddenly and joy will be completely sucked out from your soul. It was as if I am only living because I am breathing—and this is the most difficult part. I feel helpless and weak, unable to enjoy life as God has created; unable to find comfort in any big or minute thing.

Every night, I prayed the same prayer to God, "If You will, please take my life away, Lord". But every morning, I'd wake up and find myself numb, low … and still alive. For the umpteenth time, I thought about jumping off the rooftop…. The pain cannot be described. The tears cannot be hidden from myself. The screams I make as I sob sound as though I have lost a loved one. The pain depression causes is excruciating, yet numbing; sharp, yet blunt; all at the same time. It is complicated. As I type this, I am also unable to convey the feeling adequately because I am not in it now and I do not want to remember it. It is too painful to remember.

Above what depression is, depression causes me to have suicidal thoughts on quite a regular basis. Thoughts that are suicidal come and go. However, it is not every moment that I want to end my life. It is just those intricate moments when the world just seems so unbearable, distasteful and difficult that I feel that death could be the only thing that will end the misery in my mind and in my heart. In times like that, it feels as though the world will be a better place without somebody like me. My family and friends will be happier without me. My thoughts scream to me that I am a burden and unworthy of life, love and joy. The hurt I have caused people also sinks in deeper in these moments and it is amplified in my mind. I remember that I am guilty of the greatest of sins and that I am unworthy of God's love— all of these, which are true. The point is, in times like this, it is the most difficult to remember God's love and grace amidst remembering that I am a sinner, unworthy of the Almighty God to pour out Himself for me. In times like this, I forget who I am, a child of the God who has loved me from the very beginning.

I am Ruth and I have been struggling with depression all my life. It was only recently that I was officially diagnosed with this mental illness and I finally found a name that could describe what I have felt for so many years. I'm not sure why I have depression, perhaps it is a combination of genetics and my upbringing in an Asian family. I was not the closest to my family members and we oftentimes swept things that needed to be addressed under the carpet. Issues surfaced only when things escalated out of hand. Even though my family is not perfect, I love them so much. It is difficult to talk about my family but all I can say is that whilst I am the only Christian in the family, God is still good to us.

That day in the bathroom, I hit a breaking point because every attempt at trying to be a "good" or "changed" person changed nothing. My depression still stuck with me like a parasite and it sucked the life out of me. I was extremely downcast. I was furious at the Lord, questioning why He had not taken this illness away. I know that He could have but clearly had chosen not to. *My God, my God, why has Thou forsaken me?*

In an attempt to spite God for leaving me with this burden, I chose to intentionally draw away from Him. I went on dates with men regardless of their background and spent a lot of time with them instead of my church mates, friends and family—the people who really cared about me. I also began to indulge in alcohol, which seemed like a good form of distraction from thinking about God or my actions. I would often drink excessively and I always got drunk, letting myself be filled with feelings of indifference and temporal happiness. I was seeking temporary relief and anything that could numb the stinging feeling of misery in my heart. But despite my attempts, every single morning when I woke up, I would find that the pain did not go away and my heart was still as empty.

God's Persistent Pursuit of Me

Throughout that season, I still attended church, albeit with a cold heart. However, I did continue meeting a few of my closer Christian friends. When I hit my breaking point, I messaged them to say that I did not want to continue following Christ. I felt that following God and being unable to fully find joy with Him reflected that, perhaps, I am not one who is worthy of God or His love or His majesty. At the same time, I felt betrayed by the One whom I trusted most. He did not lead me to still waters and He did not give me peace. He took something very precious away from me and He has never given it back to me. Christ was neither the cause nor solution of the problem and following Christ became a burden. Without God, things would be easier. My sins will not be sins and my actions will stop angering or hurting God (at least in my mind). There was too much hurt and pain in my heart. No one could understand my circumstances. It was difficult to be me and to accept who I am—someone so broken. It was difficult to even be alive.

My friends never ever put on a holier-than-thou front or demanded that I stopped sinning. Instead, they gently reminded that I was a child of God. My close friend, Sarah, always said, "Ruth, I know you know that what you're doing is wrong in the sight of God. But, whatever you choose, just know that I will be here to support you." Other friends would also tell me how much the Lord loved me. In spite of their busy schedules, they always made time for me. They gave me time to think about things, and space to wrestle with God. They demonstrated so much love and patience, to the point where I began to see that they were how God was giving me grace to stay alive.

I still wrestle with God today, and my friends are still supporting me with prayers, words of support and loving actions. In fact, Sarah prays for me daily. Oftentimes, she texts to ask me about my progress and how I am feeling.

She takes the time to understand me and is always available whenever I need her. Above all, she has never stopped praying and trusting in the Lord for me. Sarah, and my other Christian friends, point me to the fact that Jesus is unlike any other; He is so much more secure than anything the world or people can offer.

Even in my current struggle to believe in God's goodness, I can sense that He is pursuing me. I've tried to distance myself from Him and others around me, but I can't seem to outrun Him. He turns up in the unlikeliest of places: once when my non-Christian friend told me to "go back to church", and another time when my non-Christian sister said, "God will always love you no matter what you have done or what you are feeling." These are strange things to hear from non-Christians; God really works in strange ways I cannot comprehend.

My depression makes me resonate with the writer in Psalm 88 when he wrote, "Darkness is my closest friend." (Psalm 88:18, NLT) But I know that I cannot deny God's presence or ignore His pursuit of me anymore. I have learned that the life I was running to is unfulfilling. It could never bring me the freedom and joy that I longed for. Nothing, apart from Him, could. I have decided that even if I still struggle with depression and other sins, even if I will probably fail Him time and time again, God will never forsake me, and He is worthy of my trust.

The Problem with Coming Back to Christ

However, even after I made up my mind to turn back to Him, it still took months before I gained the courage to call upon the name of Jesus again. I cannot ever erase the sins I have committed and am committing. There will never be a point whereby I will stop, as I'm in my sinful body. With all these thoughts floating in my mind, I hated myself to the core. I was the bane of my own existence and I felt like I would never be good enough for anyone in this life—not my family, friends and not God.

The turning point came when I heard a sermon on the prodigal son (Luke 15:11–32). The message got me thinking: *Was I actually afraid to turn back to God because I thought that He may not receive me with open arms anymore?* I reasoned that God knows my sin against Him on an even deeper level than my friends, family or anyone I could hide things from. How could He really want me?

When I considered the depth and weight of my sin, it was so excruciating that I found it difficult to even lift my head in front of our Holy God. But this story in Luke reminded me of God's willingness to receive me. I'm now slowly starting to grasp the truth that Christ's sacrifice on the cross is enough to cover my sin, and I stopped doubting God's forgiveness and the sacrifice Jesus made for me on the Cross.

What My Journey Means for Me Now
Although I feel like I am still at the bottom of a dark well, I hold fast to the promises of God. Just as God promised Joshua, "Do not be frightened, and do not be dismayed, for the LORD your God is with you wherever you go" (Joshua 1:9, ESV), I know that the Lord is with me even in this deep well. He brings light into my darkness, and this light allows me to see who God truly is—love. I am also assured that because of Christ, I am no longer a slave to sin, but a slave to righteousness (Romans 6:17–18). Although I may still succumb to the weakness of my flesh, I am no

longer turning my back on God, but asking Him for an obedient heart to do what pleases Him.

If you have a friend who has left the body of Christ, I want to assure you that what your friend needs is all of the love, grace, support and time he or she can get. When they don't feel like speaking to God anymore, teach him or her to pray this, "Help me, Lord, for I am a sinner." Sometimes, in a state of depression, I have nothing to say to God because I feel nothing; I also did not want to cry out to God. This prayer has helped me a lot when I felt that way and it somehow strengthens me because God is involved.

Your friend may need months, or even years, before they come back to the faith. Keep showing them God's love in the meantime, and be faithful in prayer, remembering that everything will work out—not in our timing, not in your friend's, but in *God's* perfect timing.

Another thing that the Church should take note of is to understand that a person with depression can still be faithful to God. So many times when I shared about my depression, people will be quick to say, "You need to trust in God". However, it causes me to have more self-doubt and guilt. I have been trying to trust God. And at times, I was actually close to God and His word. Depression is the cancer of the mind and it is real. Though at times it is spiritual, it is also equally physical and psychological. We need more Christians to understand this so that those with mental illness can receive the right form of help needed.

*Ruth**
Originally published on *ymi.today*. This version has been edited with permission.

HOPE FOR THE ANXIOUS MIND

It was a cold, sunny December morning in Waterloo, Ontario, in 2010. The first semester of third year was ending and exam period had arrived. For most of us students, anxiety levels were at their peak. Although my stress usually translated into motivation, something was different this time. Perhaps there was additional anxiety about my upcoming study exchange, or maybe it was the loss of some close friendships. Whatever it was, something was making this round of exams unbearable.

The weeks leading up to that December morning were also stressful. Despite many fearful thoughts, I had managed to hand in a final assignment for one class and finish an exam for another. This morning, however, my stress surpassed my ability to cope. When I woke up, my mind was whirling with a tornado of upsetting thoughts. My chest was pounding and I was overcome with fear and panic. It was as if I was falling into a dark, bottomless hole, with nothing to grasp onto. No matter what I tried, I just fell further down into the darkness and my mind raced. I was terrified. *I can't tell anyone what is in my mind*, I thought. *They'll think I'm crazy!*

But I knew I couldn't get out of this hole by myself. Even though I feared being condemned, I felt so desperate for help that I told a trusted friend everything I was thinking about. Incredibly, I received a loving and compassionate response and was reassured that everything would be fine. I was still in the dark hole, but I had stopped falling. Now, how would I get out?

That evening, I drove to my hometown to see my doctor. I was diagnosed with anxiety-related depression. I would later be excused from one exam and complete the other one the following semester. I breathed a sigh of relief. Free from school stress, I entered a sleeping marathon. In my waking hours, I tried to return to life as usual but terrorising thoughts would tauntingly push me back down. Tears riddled my days and I was grateful for moments of joy that seemed to be found only in prayer or worship. Would this be my life from now on?

Fast forward nine years to now. I have completed a Bachelor's Degree at Wilfrid Laurier University, lived in Austria, travelled Europe and Asia, lived in Vancouver, completed a Master of Arts at Regent College, met and married a Singaporean, and moved to Singapore. My days consist of work, church, cooking, reading, exercising, and spending time with new and existing friends and family.

So, what happened in the last nine years?

Understanding and Equipping

Eager to understand and manage my anxiety, I have spent hours since 2010 researching and applying various stress management techniques, and meeting with counsellors, psychiatrists and psychologists. With each experience, my condition became clearer. The conclusive diagnosis was a combination of two chronic anxiety disorders: generalised anxiety disorder (GAD) and obsessive-compulsive disorder (OCD). GAD manifests itself in higher-than-normal anxious responses to stressful situations and, more notably, to everyday situations. OCD is more diverse, taking many forms beyond the stereotypical obsession with cleanliness. OCD comprises a cycle of "obsessions", distressing or uncomfortable thoughts, and "compulsions", the actions or thoughts done to counter or escape from the obsessions. Obsessive thoughts are normally irrational and exaggerated, but to the sufferer, they seem highly legitimate. For me, both my obsessions *and* compulsions normally take the form of thoughts, i.e. my natural 'counteraction' to my obsessive thoughts is to think endlessly of ways that my fears can be mitigated.

How Does GAD/OCD Play Out in Everyday Life?
Say I have an important project deadline for work. I might have an obsessive thought like: *What if the project fails and my colleagues resent me forever?* Note the presence of "what if" (an impulse to pre-empt all the worst-case scenarios) and "forever" (the catastrophic nature of the thought)—both are staples of anxious thinking. The compulsion might begin with thoughts that sound as innocuous as this: *That's not logical. Even if the project fails, your colleagues will forgive you. You can always try a different approach. Plus, everyone will move on eventually anyway.*

Now, for those without an anxiety disorder, that line of thinking will probably be enough to dismiss the first thought (the "obsession") and allow the person to move on. However, for someone with an anxiety disorder, it becomes a compulsion that only sparks new 'what if?' scenarios or obsessions (*What if the different approach doesn't work?*, *What if they decide to hold a grudge?*, etc.). This then leads to another compulsive thought to counter the new "obsession", and so on. This endless cycle of back and forth thoughts increases anxiety levels and breeds negative feelings and emotions for the sufferer.

While the example above might seem "normal" or "mild", the person could still experience high anxiety. The level of anxiety *viscerally experienced* does not depend on the *content* of the GAD/OCD thoughts, which can range from "mild" to "disturbing". Rather, it depends on factors such as how equipped the person is to manage their experienced anxiety, how self-aware they are, whether they have a supportive community and the number of other external stressors in their life at that point.

What Has Helped You Manage the GAD/OCD that You Experience?
Learning that my condition was chronic was upsetting and difficult to accept. However, what gave me hope was the knowledge that, if well-managed, the condition would have little to no impact on my daily life. While not exhaustive, three of the most helpful handles have been:

1. My Relationship with God
I cannot express how tangible and reassuring God's presence has been in my darkest periods of anxiety and depression. Through prayer, Scripture and worship music; I have experienced God's overwhelming peace time and time again. In the worst moments, even making the simplest decision feels beyond my physical, mental and emotional capacity. The only thing I am able to do is tell God that I need His strength and grace to get out of bed and make it through the day. I am completely dependent on Him to help me, knowing that if I were to base my ability to function on how I was feeling, I would not be able to do it.

True to His Word, God comes through for me every single time. The ways in which He meets me are so varied—from prompting a friend to get in touch and cheer me up, to opening my eyes to little blessings that He is giving me—but each is timely and specific to the need I have in that moment, and gives me the strength to keep taking small steps forward. Days that started out feeling impossible to get through would end up becoming testimonies of His faithfulness to me.

2. A Supportive Community of Family and Friends

One of the best answers to my prayers for God's grace has been the community that He has provided to journey with me. The ability to process my experience with trusted friends and family without judgement has given me the strength to persevere.

When I experience intense anxiety, it often feels like I will never know joy again. The vortex of thoughts and emotions is so strong that I feel the deepest hopelessness imaginable. In the darkest times when I am overcome by despair, I withdraw from people. A flood of tears flows from my tightly clenched eyes. If I am at home at a time like this, I often retreat into my room, lay on my bed, and try to understand and unpack my thoughts. While these bring immediate comfort, they also sustain and even feed anxious thinking. The cocktail of ingredients—depressive physical posture, isolating myself, and focusing all my attention on my thoughts—simply continues the spiral.

But by God's grace, I am not fighting alone. I am grateful for my husband who has a miraculous ability to help me help myself. When I reach my darkest points, my husband reminds me to ground myself. He says things like, "Look at your surroundings. Open your eyes. Where are you? What do you see?", which forces me to shift my focus from my inner world to the larger external surrounding. As I re-enter my physical surroundings, slowly but surely, he encourages me to change my physical posture from lying down to sitting or standing. This simple process of awareness is remarkably effective for me in kick-starting the recalibration process, dissolving despair and returning me to a healthy thinking space.

To further counteract the downward spiral, my husband prompts me to verbalise my anxious thoughts. Externalising what I am feeling keeps me from ruminating on my thoughts. It has also helped him understand what I grapple with, to the point where he can even estimate how long each anxiety cycle will take! "You'll be okay in about 45 minutes after you cry it out," he tells me. It is unexpectedly comforting to hear that, because it reminds me that this acute anxiety has parameters and is not an overwhelming and endless abyss that I will never be able to get out of.

After the anxiety cycle is over, we try to reflect on what the triggers were, identify patterns between cycles, and think about handles to help with the next cycle. As I do this with my husband or trusted family or friends, not only are their collective ideas and feedback insightful, but their support is without judgement and thus empowering—it reminds me that I am not a helpless victim of my circumstances and have the ability to shape my life. While the anxiety that I feel may be something I cannot control, I can choose how I respond to it by finding ways to overcome my struggles with the help of people who care about me.

3. Cognitive Behavioural Therapy (CBT)

Going for therapy has also been instrumental in recovering from GAD and OCD. One of the most effective therapies for me and many others with anxiety disorders is CBT.[1] CBT training involves identifying negative patterns and creating a plan of action to overcome them, all with the guidance of a trained counsellor. Through a variety of structured techniques and strategies, I have reaped the benefits of CBT, experiencing significant correcting of my thoughts, emotions and behaviours.

How Can the Church Support GAD/OCD Sufferers?

In 2016, the Institute of Mental Health (IMH) completed the Singapore Mental Health Study (SMHS), the most recent in Singapore to date. Done in collaboration with the Ministry of Health (MOH) and Nanyang Technological University (NTU), the study showed that 1 in 28 Singaporeans experience OCD, making it the third most common mental illness after major depressive disorder (1 in 16) and alcohol abuse (1 in 24).[2] The study also showed that 1 in 7 people in Singapore experience mental illness in their lifetime.[3]

---

1   This website offers useful exercises and resources for an introduction to CBT: "25 CBT Techniques and Worksheets for Cognitive Behavioral Therapy." *PositivePsychology.com*. June 19, 2019. Accessed July 03, 2019. https://positivepsychology.com/cbt-cognitive-behavioral-therapy-techniques-worksheets/.

2   Baker, Jalelah Abu. "OCD One of the Most Common Mental Disorders in Singapore." *CNA*. December 11, 2018. Accessed June 12, 2019. https://www.channelnewsasia.com/news/singapore/ocd-one-of-the-most-common-mental-disorders-in-singapore-11020354.

3   Institute of Mental Health, 2005. "Latest nationwide study shows 1 in 7 people in Singapore has experienced a mental disorder in their lifetime." https://www.imh.com.sg/uploadedFiles/Newsroom/News_Releases/SMHS%202016_Media%20Release_FINAL_web%20upload.pdf.

If we apply these statistics to churches, it is likely that almost every person has either wrestled with mental illness themselves, or knows someone who has. If we truly believe that one person's suffering will impact the larger church, how can the church family help?

1. Church staff and pastors can learn about OCD, GAD, and other mental illnesses via short courses or workshops conducted by experts in the field.

2. They can then educate their congregation so that the church community as a whole can learn how to be more supportive of those with mental illnesses.

3. They can introduce programmes like Support Groups where a trained therapist meets with groups of those suffering with the same mental illness (i.e. OCD sufferers) so they can receive structured training and encourage and pray for one another so they do not feel alone.

4. If it is within their means, churches can offer subsidised professional counselling/psychological services. Those with mental illnesses often need to pay for regular check-ups, medication and enough counselling sessions to stabilise their condition. Subsidised assistance would significantly alleviate the sufferer's financial burden and, consequently, additional stress.

Moving Forward
While anxiety is a result of the Fall, thankfully, that is not where our story ends. Our redemptive God wants to restore creation and this includes restoring us to the people we were created to be: "Therefore, if anyone is in Christ, the new creation has come: The old has gone, the new is here!" (2 Corinthians 5:17).

To those helping people with mental illness:
You are partners of God, bringing restoration and shalom to all of creation. May God grant you wisdom to encourage, patience to listen, His heart to love without judgement and hope that He has everything in His loving hands.

To those suffering with anxiety or OCD, or any other mental illness:
Hope: Do not lose hope and *never ever* give up. Nothing is ever too bad to give up the beautiful gift of life. This too shall pass.

Assurance: Remember that you are not crazy, and you *can* live a normal life. It will take hard work but you will grow stronger and stronger.

Share: Remember that you are not alone. *Please* reach out to counsellors, psychiatrists, psychologists, trusted friends or trusted family members. Be as transparent as you can so you can receive the most beneficial help.

Rest: Rest in the knowledge that God is holding you, even if it doesn't seem like it at times. He loves you and will use your life in ways you cannot imagine. You've got this because God's got you.

Shoni Duesling

LESSONS FROM THE BRINK
– *Reflection* –

Introduction
One thing that strikes you about the stories in this section is the variety of the folks who are sharing their stories. Men and women, young and old, new believers and mature Christian leaders, highly educated and those with minimal formal education—they have all been afflicted with one type of mental illness or another. Their stories are a stark reminder that we all live in a fallen world and we all experience brokenness in one way or another.

Mental illness, however, has not received the same attention in the Church as other forms of brokenness. The Church is more familiar with moral failures. Mature churches would have ways to help members who have sinned to repent and be restored. As for illnesses, most churches would also have some way to manage physical illnesses; usually some combination of prayer and medical treatment.

However, mental illness represents a special challenge because the church's usual healing approaches assume that the person needing healing can rationally understand the treatments proposed and can cooperate in their healing. What happens when a person's thinking is compromised and he or she can't fully understand what is happening to them or why they should be treated in a certain way?

Stigma and Quick Fixes

Some of the stories speak of a stigma against those who suffer from mental illness. This sense of a stigma may be partially imagined. But in a society like Singapore's where Confucian values are still influential, there is still a sense of shame associated with mental illness. This makes it hard for people to seek help. It may also lead to a sense of denial from the person's community. This compounds the pain, loneliness and despair that the person is already experiencing.

And since mental illness is something that is socially embarrassing, people may suggest quick fixes to help one "get over" one's mental illness. There are spiritual quick fixes—pray more, read the Bible, worship. Or there are medical quick fixes—visit the right counsellor or psychiatrist and they will set you right. But a quick-fix approach is unhelpful at best and may actually be harmful.

Reading the stories, it is clear that each person is different and how each experiences his or her struggle is different. The different types of mental illness are also different. Depression is different from anxiety attacks, which is different from schizophrenia. There is no spiritual or medical silver bullet that can cure a person of mental illness effectively and quickly. Each person and each condition is different. If the Church is serious about compassionately helping those who struggle with mental illness, it must be prepared to invest time, money, energy and attention to be really helpful.

We are not suggesting that prayer, Bible study, Christian community and worship do not help. Reading the stories, there were times when they did. What we need to be wary of is a one-size-fits-all approach that assumes all cases of mental illness can be easily healed with the usual spiritual disciplines.

A word here about those who believe that mental illness is caused by evil spirits. All Bible-believing Christians believe in Satan and the malevolent spirits under his authority and there are times when demonic spirits may afflict a person. It may be wise for an interdisciplinary team to manage some cases.

Even if evil spirits are involved, it is usually some pre-existing brokenness in a person that makes that person vulnerable to mental illness. But demonic involvement should be the last thing we look for, not the first. We do not help anyone by casting out imaginary spirits from them when what they really need is good psychiatric care.

The Power of Love
A common theme in the stories is how the intervention of caring individuals made a key difference in how people moved towards healing. There are a number of ways we can show love to those afflicted by mental illness.

A love that accepts
We begin by accepting folks as they are. Yes, we want them to get better, but first they must know that they are loved as they are.

A love that understands
Next, love must be expressed in the willingness to walk with those suffering from mental illness, to help understand what they are actually suffering from. If the illness is severe this will surely include seeking professional help.

A love that supports

Usually, serious mental illness will not be cured immediately. To love is to provide as best we can what the person needs: spiritually, emotionally, financially, etc. This may mean mobilising various agencies—family, church, governmental bodies. Depending on how the person heals, a commitment to support could be a long-term one. We also need to recognise that some illnesses may only be fully healed in the new heavens and the new earth.

Faith and Science

One of the contributors to this section, Dr George Khoo, is both a medical doctor and church elder. He makes a strong case for the fact that if medications like anti-depressants are needed, we should take them. Indeed, we should not see the use of medications as a betrayal of our faith in the Lord. There are some in the Christian community who believe that if we trust the Lord to heal, we shouldn't need medications. This is erroneous thinking. Medicines work because they function based on the laws of science that the Lord has put in place to run the universe. God can and does heal miraculously and directly. But, usually, He heals through medicines and medical procedures that He has allowed humankind to discover in His wonderful creation. What is needed of course is to consult competent doctors who will give good medical care. Ultimately, our trust is not in the doctors and the medicines. Indeed, some of the stories show the limits of medical science. Our trust is in the Lord but we welcome doctors and medicines as His servants.

Growth

What is particularly encouraging in the stories is to see how the contributors have grown through their struggles.

The fact that they can now write their stories shows that they are in a place where they can reflect and learn from their pain. Going through their valleys has enabled them to grow in their personal maturity and in their walk with God. Such growth cannot be assumed. The contributors, often with the help of caring friends and family, have allowed their pains and struggles to shape their lives positively. What is particularly encouraging is that a number of them now want to use what lessons they have learnt through their journeys to help others similarly afflicted. They are in a unique position to do so because of their ability to empathise and to help with understanding.

The Road Ahead

The pace of modern life in general and the unique stresses of life in Singapore mean that we will continue to encounter people who struggle with mental illness both in the Church and in the wider society. We are told that numbers are expected to rise. People will grapple with different types of mental illness and in various severities. If the Church is truly a good news community it must be committed to extending God's love to those who suffer from mental illness. We look forward to the day when there will be no more illness (Revelation 21). Until that day, we extend God's care to all who need it.

Tan Soo-Inn
Chairman
Graceworks Private Limited

SECTION 2 — WALKING WITH THE WOUNDED

HOW GOD SAVED MY SCHIZOPHRENIC MOTHER (AND ME)

My mother was diagnosed with Schizophrenia even before I was born. So throughout my childhood, my family centred our lives around her condition. As an only child, I learned to live in a silent house where telephones and televisions were banned, move to a new place just to avoid neighbours, and hide in the shadows if my mother was having an 'episode'.

Growing up, I was aware that things at home were not normal. But since I did not know what 'normal' looked like, I tried to live as normally as I could. I had little contact with the external world and not many social skills. I didn't tell anyone what I was going through; nobody talked about such things with a little kid either. I sought escape through reading—the one form of media that was allowed at home. I was able to live freely and create worlds that were not under the control of someone else. I found myself sleeping whenever possible to avoid having to spend time with my mother.

My mother would often tell me that she loved me. And I knew she did. She cared for me by dictating what was 'good' or 'right' for me, but with little input from me. For instance, I was often only given one type of food for all my meals (like bread or fish) because she strongly believed it was 'healthy for me'. As a result, there were many moments I would wonder, "Why does this love feel so painful? If this is love, I'd much rather live without it."

Although my mother's condition meant she could only show me inconsistent displays of love, my father was the constant in both our lives. He was a backslidden Christian at the point that he married my mother—but he held fast to his faith in his heart. He told me before that he felt that the Holy Spirit had assured him to "take care of this woman for the rest of your life".

As the sole breadwinner, he was consistent in his message to me of what love looked like—both in words and actions. When things got difficult because of work, finances and a volatile home environment, he would lose his temper just like anyone else. Yet, he never wavered in his conviction to stand by my family and my mother. For him, marrying my mother was a step of faith and obedience to God, and that conviction helped him to stay in the marriage when my mother was unwell. He protected us to the best of his ability. I believe a lot of my resilience and ability to cope came from him.

One day, when I was about seven, my father decided to bring me to Sunday school. I went grudgingly. I remember the room being very spacious and filled with light, smiling faces and music. I thought to myself, "These people are crazy. Why are they so happy?" Because their happiness felt so distant, I felt awkward and uncomfortable and refused to go back to Sunday school a second time. My father didn't push me either.

During my secondary school years, I had a classmate who was very intent on inviting everyone she met to attend church services. My friends and I used to talk behind her back about this. But because of her persistence, a few of us eventually decided to join her for a church service.

At the church, I saw people raising their hands and singing. I had never felt that sense of warmth before from the many years of going to the temple with my mother. It was a different and uncomfortable feeling—and it freaked me out. I remember turning to my friend after the church service and telling her, "You guys are a cult. I am never coming back to your church again."

Interestingly, a few weeks after attending the church service, my father came to me and said, "We have something to tell you. Mummy has decided to accept Jesus Christ and become a Christian." Immediately, the thought that came to my mind was, "This has nothing to do with me. Tell me for what?" But of course, I knew better than to say that. Instead, I replied, "Orh."

A couple of days later, my mother had a psychotic episode (where one experiences delusions and hallucinations). My father and I tried to pacify her and explain that the fear that she was experiencing was not rational. She replied that we were out to harm her as well. Though hurt and helpless at her delusion and accusation, my father said to her, "Why don't you pray to God and ask Him what He thinks?"

To my surprise, she complied and bowed her head to pray. After a long two minute silence, she lifted her head and said, "God told me what I'm doing now is *not right*."

Nothing could describe how I felt when I heard those words. Did my mother just admit that she was wrong? Throughout my entire life, my mother would insist on her way whenever she was experiencing psychosis until we gave in. But this time, something (or someone) got through to her.

From that day onwards, things changed at home. There were still frequent arguments and breakdowns, but I stopped seeing objects fly around the house. My mother started to acknowledge her need to take her medication and apologize when she behaved in a hurtful manner.

Not only did her delusions subside, but her relationship with us also improved because God showed her how to love. Through that, I witnessed the Spirit of the living God in her, teaching her that His love and power are greater than her thoughts and fears.

As a result, my heart changed as well. I began to trust more, and open up more. Eventually, I started to attend church with my parents. Over time, God worked in my heart and helped me see the truth of his existence and goodness, which I was finally convinced of when He healed the calluses on my hand after a week of praying beside my windowsill every night.

In hindsight, I can trace the miracle that God had done for my family. He healed my parents and me with His unwavering steadfast love—despite all those times I had rejected Him when I stepped into churches.

That, however, was not the end of the journey, as my family continued to go through different seasons of learning. The church community was well intentioned, but the mixed bag of advice we received was not always helpful. My mother was encouraged by her church friends to "have faith in God for healing, don't rely on medication". So she began to reduce the dosage on her own and eventually stopped taking her medication completely, which led to a major relapse. Thankfully, because of the care of the Institute of Mental Health doctors for my mother, she was able to recover from that episode.

To me, advice about how faith in God can heal can be detrimental to those who experience partial healing like how my mother did when she accepted Christ. Just because we do not see immediate healing does not mean that we do not have faith in God; it may just mean that God has a different plan for our lives. From my family's experience, taking medication regularly and receiving good consultation from doctors was and continues to be an essential part of the journey for my mother to hear the Holy Spirit clearly daily, without confusion.

One thing I have learnt from the doctors, as well as the church community, is that consistency is key to helping those with mental health diagnoses. This can come in the form of regularly spending time together, or praying together, or doing activities together. You never know how God can use our consistency through darkness to bring light.

The journey may have been painful, but it has been so beautiful to witness first-hand God's presence to mend our broken lives. I will always be grateful to Jesus for being willing to do what no one else was able or willing to do, which is to reach out His hand to my family and save us—even me.

*Alice**

WHEN I REALISED HE HAD ANXIETY

It started with a common cold. It became a protracted flu and he began to complain about losing his sense of taste. We all thought it was just the sickness, but then the flu passed and his taste buds still hadn't revived. At the time, I was in the first semester of my first year in tertiary education and so spent a lot of my time out of the house—weekends included. This meant that I charted his worsening condition through the dinner conversations we had on the rare occasion I was home early. He would complain about the apparent blandness of the food. Because of that, he started to eat less, and even talk less. It didn't matter how many of his favourite dishes my mother cooked, he couldn't seem to taste them and his mood only got worse. I didn't want to think about it at the time. I was more concerned with handling my own problems; balancing my time between school, friends, and hobbies. I thought he would pull out of it soon enough, and that maybe he was just stressed.

So I didn't know exactly when my father started to struggle with anxiety, or when he stopped being able to work for a while. Honestly, I only really registered that he was having trouble when my mother told me one day that my father was going through a tough time and that we needed to support him through it. Even then, I don't think I took it too seriously.

It was lunchtime on one of the weekends that I happened to be home. I left my room intending to ask what my father wanted for lunch. I saw him sitting in a chair looking into blank space, his hand clutching his chest. He looked up at me when he realised I was there and said,

"I can't breathe."

He repeated it in a breathy voice, as if gasping for air. He said something about his heart racing, beating so fast, that he might need an ambulance. What is this, he asked, what was happening?

I realised what was going on. I moved back a little, giving him more space and then told him, "Listen to me. Listen to me, you're having a panic attack. Just breathe. Breathe. I'm going to count, breathe with me. One, inhale. Two, three, four, five. Exhale, one, two, three ..."

We continued like this for a while until he stopped hyperventilating. We were silent as he recomposed himself. He asked me how I had known what to do. I explained that it wasn't the first time that I had to help someone through a panic attack; that it wasn't uncommon among my friends to deal with stuff like that. He was surprised, and said he had no idea.

I never mentioned it because I never had a reason to. It wasn't strange to me either. There have been so many reports about how mental illness is on the rise among today's youth, it seems to have become the norm. But despite that, it felt strange having to interact with my father when he was in that state, to be the one who knew what was going on and how to navigate through it. It was painful. When someone slips and falls down you can run to them and help them up, support them physically, and show empathy in that way. Helping someone through a panic attack is a much more emotionally separating experience. There are no wounds for you to help dress; it is a battle that they alone must fight.

That was the episode that made me realise he was dealing with something serious and that it wouldn't just "go away". That wasn't the only panic attack that I would have to help him through. Another time, he rapped on my bedroom door asking me for help, his voice in that same higher register and his hand gripping his chest. I counted and we breathed. We had moved to the same room as that first time and were sitting in the same positions.

After he recovered sufficiently, he asked me if I thought he was weak. I told him it wasn't a matter of being strong or weak, and that it could happen to anyone. A learned response—the same I had given to a friend. It felt odd having to say that to my father, and give the kind of reassurance that usually comes from the caretaker. I don't think he ever had to think about anxiety and depression in relation to himself before, and navigating it was an entirely new experience to him. Seeing me being more familiar with the situation he was going through than he was, also discomforted him.

During the time he was still trying to figure out what exactly was happening to him, little was said during my family's dinner conversations. He had always been somewhat talkative at the dinner table so the change was disconcerting. Those meals became too short, with the silence filled only by the sound of tableware. Sometimes my father didn't come out to eat at all. We would usually hang around the dinner table and living room after meals to chat for a while, but during that period I would retreat to my room immediately after I had finished my food.

But once my parents came to terms with the situation, they spent mealtimes discussing the different ways of cheering him up, or helping him get a good night's sleep. At first, each meal would be punctuated with her asking if he could taste the food. Later on, he asked that she stop, saying, "If I taste anything, I will tell you." He hadn't gotten much better yet, but he was starting to find his way to recovery. I kept quiet for most of this, not feeling comfortable offering an opinion. I don't know if he would have felt better if I had tried to help, or felt relieved that I was able to continue on normally when he was in such a state. So instead, I just prayed and trusted that he would find a way to get better. But there was one occasion when I did lend my voice.

He was having a particularly bad day and was musing aloud at the dinner table, asking himself the same question over and over again. He kept coming back to the fact that he was finding it so difficult to manage his condition. "Why", he asked, "why is it so hard for me to handle this?" He was a confident middle-aged man and it must have bothered him a great deal that he was finding such difficulty in the situation. After hearing him ponder this for the whole duration of the meal, I couldn't help but feel the need to try to give an answer. So I said, "That's because this is an entirely new experience for you. You're like a child that's fallen down for the first time. For others watching, it's something so small, but for you it's like the world is ending. Because it's something you've never dealt with before. And just because it's easy for someone else doesn't make your difficulty any smaller. Because you are having to navigate that for the first time yourself."

I bit back tears and stronger emotions, picked up my empty plate and headed to the kitchen. Behind me, I heard him say, "Wow. I never saw it like that." I nodded, and returned a short "Yeah." He would tell me later that my words at the time were really impactful for him and it made me feel glad to have been able to help in such a way.

Sometime later over a meal, I found out that he had visited a psychiatrist. My parents were discussing the various things that they had been told, one of which was the possibility that he could be put on medication. Eventually, my mother asked for my opinion on whether I thought he should take the medicine. I thought about the experiences my friends have had—becoming reliant on that supposedly short-term solution and wanting to stop but being unable to do so. I observed how different they could be on or off medication and how uncomfortable I felt doubting them, wondering if they were acting a certain way because of the medicine they were taking.

I told my parents I wouldn't want my father to be put on medication, but if they thought it was the best option, to then go for it. I was worried that he wouldn't be the same again even if he got better as he would have become reliant on the medication. At the same time, if the medication was something he needed, I didn't want to get in the way. They made that decision some days later, and he started taking it. I remember the way he described how immediate the relief felt. To him, it was like he had seen light for the first time in months. Indeed when he spoke, I started to see the person I had always known. It was up and down from there; he had good and bad days—which was an improvement from when he was in the throes of his condition. The medicine gave him a reprieve that allowed him to start addressing his problems. So despite my misgivings, I became thankful for it. Things started to get better after this, we started going out as a family again—something we had stopped doing as crowds triggered his anxiety—and he was able to progressively regain more of his normal life.

Recovery came gradually and soon everything returned—starting with his sense of taste. It returned in parts and he would narrate the ways that he rediscovered the food that he loved. He would describe how the sweetness had returned but the savoury was still faint, still eluding him. I still remember the joy with which he described the taste of rice, and how happy he was to be able to taste plain rice. His ability to find joy in that simple thing was reassurance that he had really gotten better. If his first panic attack was when I accepted that he was dealing with mental illness, him tasting rice again was when I marked his recovery.

I consider my father fortunate to have gone through that period of time so quickly when I think of friends around my age who still actively deal with issues like anxiety or depression, and have done so for years of their lives now. Mental health problems can come in many forms and anyone, at any point of their life, can suffer from them. Although there has been less stigma these days around talking about it and seeking help, everyone has a different experience with those close to them and there is still room for improvement. All of us can be more accepting and understanding of our loved ones in these times, and be ready to offer whatever help we can. It might be hard to always embody the ideal level of supportiveness we want to give but every moment counts. And as I've found, sometimes it only takes a few words to help them along in their journey.

Myer Wong

NB: Read Myer's father, Mike's story on page 1 and his mother, Wong Moy Yin's story on page 115.

HELPLESSNESS OF THE HELPER

I began my tertiary education in social work because of many reasons, but the primary one was to combat the pervasive feelings I had of being a failure. I felt helpless when it came to helping others and wanted to know how to help others better (or at least, help). I had friends I had tried to help, heal and encourage—but failed. All my efforts so far had been futile.

Friend: You're a bigot, you know.

Me: Why? I am just trying to tell you that this Jesus way might really be what you need.

Friend: That's bigotry.

In retrospect, I was just a young and foolish teenager who was too zealous to help. Too quick to dish out "great" thoughts and words of positivity and hope. I so desired to be that shining light in this dark world. If only I knew how to use the right words, better phrase them, maybe I could have magically helped someone. I did improve along the way, from saying "Don't worry" to "God hears your prayers", albeit at the wrong time. And there it started, my unquenchable desire to equip myself with more skills and theories to help others. I slapped on education upon education; courses upon courses. The futility remained.

Years down the road, armed with more and more letters behind my name, knowledge didn't help my feelings of inadequacy. Friends, clients, and patients, never seemed to get better the way I imagined they should. Even when they improved, I remained anxious. "Would they relapse? When?" I would wonder. Some said, "Some people are lost causes, don't blame yourself", or "Have faith, everything will be okay". Others said, "Maybe they will get better later." Some others said it was the countertransference (feelings a helper has in response to the person we are trying to help) that made me feel helpless. Yet in many ways, this has helped me to empathise with the depths of helplessness the other person might be feeling. So I continued to unpack and muddle through any feelings of helplessness with my supervisors and peers.

It continues to be a painful process, hopefully a painful progress too. But more often than not, we parallel the people we want to help—one step forward, two steps back. So, there we go, pain upon pain; self-judgement upon self-judgement.

By then, I knew nothing really worked to shake off the feelings of helplessness. Though research showed that certain interventions work for certain types of issues (e.g. interpersonal psychotherapy for those with depression, family interventions for those with eating disorders), evidence also does show that help is not always helpful. No matter how good my help is, it can have negative side effects. Help can be painful, receiving help can cause a narcissistic injury. Interventions can be triggers too. Opening a can of worms of historical pain and not closing the can in time is unhelpful to one's short-term functioning. To receive help is to say "I can't do it" and to leave with the same—or worse—feelings one had in the beginning. Wow. That is how sometimes things pan out. So it is no wonder, that I had this conversation with a peer.

Me: I think I don't want to see her anymore.

Peer: Oh.

Me: Can I not see her?

Peer: But why?

Me: I think she gets very triggered and gets worse whenever she sees me! She gets worse you know.

Peer: For now she might be triggered, but in the long run, who knows?

No doubt, I can rationalize away those negative feelings. Or I can also use these feelings to help myself understand how the other person has been feeling. But the solution is inadequate. I am inadequate. Inadequacy upon inadequacy, pain upon pain. The futility is almost painful.

But the worst blow is when hope for the future is lost. When a suicidal person successfully completes his/her desire. When someone runs away or hides. What help can I give? What hope can I give if I myself resonate with the same hopelessness?

Friend: How are you?

Me: I am tired, like really tired.

Friend: Do you think maybe you are burnt out?

Me: Can't really afford to be burnt out at this point in time though. But you are probably right. Patient died.

Friend: Oh, why?

Me: Erm, people die, you know right?

And there, the story repeats. People die—both in real life and in our minds. Every goodbye, every termination of a helping relationship, every death. With that, bit by bit, hope is washed away with every untimely termination or unsatisfactory outcome. Even good terminations—when someone gets well enough and no longer needs my help—are anxiety provoking. Can this person do without further help? Termination upon termination; losses upon losses. The futility is now overwhelming.

The kicker came when my own eventual burnout came. Sometimes the feeling was transient and at times, longer than needed, or maybe, as long as needed. Once, I laid in bed, motionless, thinking about my patient. I cried. Her story was too painful. I couldn't get up. And then there was the here-to-stay-for-a-while burnout that comes when my personal life takes a hit. But the most salient one was when a trusted person betrayed me out of the blue. I could barely function on a day-to-day basis and had to allow myself to get help when I could not help myself.

I felt the mocking crowd inside me saying, "If you are the helper, help yourself!" The abyss went deeper. And here, these verses floated up to seemingly remind me, that what I was experiencing too, is for a reason: "Blessed be the God and Father of our Lord Jesus Christ, the Father of mercies and God of all comfort, who comforts us in all our affliction, so that we may be able to comfort those who are in affliction, with the comfort with which we ourselves are comforted by God." (2 Corinthians 1:3–4, ESV) You mean I had to endure pain just so that I could be a better helper? It felt meaningless! Why can't we all have slightly more palatable lives?

Still, it was faith that God could take all the negativity in me, that God would not find the hopelessness disdainful, that carried me through those dark days.

So here I am. Sensing the meaninglessness of trying to help others and knowing I can't really help myself sometimes. Yet, I've also come to realize, two is better than one. I rode on the hope of others: The gentle pacing of a friend. The confronting words of a therapist. The spirit-filled music of an anointed minister.

Whatever I needed to move ahead, I received.

To be sure, I still feel a sense of helplessness. But it is no longer meaningless. This helplessness reminds me of how I cannot do everything. So I stay with this helplessness. And that is okay.

Sophie Cheng

HE AIN'T HEAVY, HE'S MY BROTHER

Bruce* and I have been close friends for over a decade. It was around 2010 that his struggle with depression and anxiety started. We had just completed our National Service and were at a crossroad. While most of our friends were preparing to enter university, Bruce was experiencing anxiety and a lack of direction. During this time, we met up fairly often and had several heart-to-heart talks (HTHTs).

"Bro, I don't know why God put me in this position," he began, while we were catching up at the hawker centre near our church one day.

"What do you mean, bro?" I asked.

"Others seem to have such a smooth life—studies, work, relationships—whereas I have nothing going right for me. I don't know what to do with my life, and I'm afraid of making mistakes. I'm constantly worried about how others would perceive me." he explained.

Whenever we had our HTHTs, our conversations centred mainly on both our struggles and encouragement for one another, and it was not uncommon to hear one another share about these real and raw struggles. In that season, we were both serving as youth leaders in church and we were accountable to one another and our leaders. Having these HTHTs was our way of supporting and sharpening one another (Proverbs 27:17).

But the year 2012 was the breaking point for Bruce. He was studying in a local university then, when he decided to transfer to a different university to study another course he deemed more suitable. As Bruce did not meet one of the course requirements, he had to take a bridging course. However, he failed the exam of the bridging course. That was when the downward spiral started.

"I'm such a failure," Bruce lamented.

Since he was not able to study the course he wanted, he decided to work instead to make ends meet. Being the eldest child in the family, Bruce felt pressured to financially support his elderly parents. On top of his failure to enter the new course, another contributing factor to his sense of self-loathing was the rejection he faced when he pursued a romantic interest in church.

With each setback that Bruce faced, I observed how he would ruminate on the situations that reinforced his perceived identity as a failure. I noticed how some of these unhealthy thoughts festered, but as he shared his honest thoughts and feelings during our HTHT sessions, all I could do was be his listening ear.

While chewing may ease a cow's digestion, it did the opposite for Bruce's mental health. By 2013, his mental health had deteriorated. His negative narrative soon turned into suicidal thoughts, and he struggled with the latter daily. He wanted to end the pain once and for all, and entertained thoughts of jumping off a HDB block. However, he was also keenly aware that if he did not die, he would be in a worse physical state while still suffering emotionally. He also confided in me that he had contemplated the thought of using a weapon during his reservist to end his life. All this while, I found myself increasingly burdened and even exhausted after listening to his sharing. Only on hindsight did I realise it was because I was trying to tend to his wounds by my own strength.

At one point, I tried to invite him back into our church's young adults' community (he had not been plugged in for some time) so that more of our friends could share his burdens. However, it was not long after that he isolated himself from the community, fearing that others would view him negatively. On these occasions, he would express feelings of hopelessness and helplessness—despite countless reassurances.

"Paul, God is unfair to me. I have been dealt with a bad hand in my life!" Bruce snapped, during one of our regular HTHTs.

I sat there with a heavy heart, uncertain of the right words to say. This was not the first time I had heard him lash out with these words. All I could do was simply listen and offer a word of prayer. I remembered several occasions when I broke down in tears, broken and frustrated at how this brother could not see beyond the negativity. It was during times like these that I turned desperately to Jesus and cried out for help. I knew I could not do this on my own. I prayed on multiple nights for God's mercy and grace to be upon this dear brother who was hurting inside. God's assurance came in the form of reminders from His word. As in Matthew 11:28–30, I held to the promise that He will give me rest when I was feeling weary and burdened. God assured me that His yoke is easy and light and that I did not have to carry it all on my own even as I was trying to be of support to someone else.

Seeking Help

It is never easy to tell someone you care for deeply that they require professional psychiatric support. Bruce feared the stigma. He feared that seeking professional help would be a stumbling block to his future, making it difficult for him to find jobs in the future or to find someone who could accept him for who he is.

I was somewhat familiar with the stigma given that I was majoring in Psychology then. But by God's grace and with some gentle prompting, Bruce sought professional help; he simply knew that he did not want to go on living like this. Just when I thought that we had overcome the greatest hurdle, I was proven wrong. The journey itself proved to be more challenging than I had expected.

For one, there were the unhelpful comments from well-intentioned loved ones who did not think that seeking professional help was the best solution. Though his mother was not against Bruce's decision to seek professional help, she appeared reluctant. She tried to understand what depression was in her own ways, but one of her statements affected Bruce greatly. On one occasion, she blurted out: "Oh, just don't think about these negative thoughts. You just need to snap out of it!"

During church services, my friends and I would encourage him to seek healing from God. He also visited his uncle's church and during one of the healing services, he heard the same message he had heard from us, "Believe, and you will be healed!"

Over time, I saw Bruce questioning those closest to him, even me as his brother. "Bro, I believe, and I want to be healed! But why am I still not healed of my depression? Why do I feel that God is unjust? Why do non-Christians appear to have a better life than I do? Does God not love me?" he asked me once.

Bruce shared that being told by church friends and leaders that he needed more faith and that he would just need to receive the gift of the Holy Spirit was very damaging to him. Being advised to "pray it away" was most unhelpful to him. He started to doubt that God was even listening to his prayers. He felt he was cursed and short-changed. It was as though Bruce was wearing a pair of apocalyptic glasses where his situation appeared futile and pointless to him. To Bruce, God was indifferent and distant to him; God cared for others and not him. God's promises that would bring hope and life were bleak and dead to Bruce.

Those who knew Bruce superficially did not know of his deepest struggles. On the exterior, Bruce would try to look his best, like things were all in order. He would go to work normally and take a half-day leave each month to see a psychiatrist. His bosses and colleagues did not pry into that, which he appreciated. In church, he shared about his struggles only with a small group of us, as he did not know how others might view his situation. Bruce also attempted to share with others he trusted, but many did not know how to react after he shared what he was going through. He admitted that despite his calm appearance, he felt he was dying inside. It was almost as if he yearned for others to understand what he was going through. There was no doubt that the overwhelming negative feelings he had were real. I could only pray that Jesus would reveal Himself to Bruce and comfort him during his darkest moments. And Jesus did answer in His own time and way.

Good News?
Since I started journeying with Bruce, we have both attained new milestones in life. I have embarked on my career as a psychologist, and in 2015, Bruce received an academic award for his studies—I was especially proud of him for that achievement. I thanked God for His grace upon Bruce, helping him come a long way since 2012. Identifying his strengths, and celebrating small milestones was our way of encouraging him. It was moments like this that reminded me of 1 Corinthians 12:26, which says that "If one part (of the body of Christ) suffers, every part suffers with it; if one part is honoured, every part rejoices with it".

Though Bruce is coping better with his battle with depression and anxiety symptoms today, I sense his growing bitterness and resentment towards God and with some church members. Despite the hurdles he has crossed, he still feels that he would not be in such a "bad state" if God were really there. Though it pains me that he has recently left the faith and now identifies as an atheist (at the point of writing), I still pray for him regularly and hold on to the verses from Romans 8:38–39. In this passage, the Apostle Paul reminds us that we are not immune from trouble, hardship, persecution, famine, nakedness, danger, or sword, but that in the midst of all these things, nothing will be able to separate us from the love of God that is in Christ Jesus our Lord.

Whether church member, friend, family member, or a spouse; you may be wondering how to care for someone you love. In the question lies the answer: you simply *love* them. Loving Bruce meant being present for him. Sometimes all it took was being silent and listening, especially when it felt like he was not responding to such support (being present, giving a listening ear, sitting with him). Bruce would confide in me that advice-giving was not helpful at all. The worst was when someone did not listen and yet pretended to understand him. What he appreciated was a safe space to share his honest experiences in his own dark tunnel.

It has been many years of struggle in my walk with this friend, but this journey has only brought me closer to God and deepened my friendship with Bruce.

To my brother, Bruce, this is what I'd like to say: *Bruce, when Christ returns, I know your tears will be wiped away and you will be restored. For now, please know that you are loved, you are held, and you will be sustained.*

Paul Yong

WHEN A HURTING PERSON IS HURT BY THE CHURCH

I will never forget the day I received a call from my friend who had just attempted suicide. It was during one of my most difficult semesters of university and I was in the midst of preparing for my finals. It was in the middle of the night that Paige* had called me out of the blue. Under those stressful circumstances, I wasn't intending to pick up the call. But something told me that it must be urgent if not she would not be calling me so suddenly. So I answered the phone. True enough, Paige told me that she had just slit her wrists. Stunned, I dropped everything I was doing at that moment and looked for a quiet place to talk to her.

At the time, she was overseas, and I was in Singapore. So all I could do was to keep her on the line and hear her out, hoping that she would not do anything else to harm herself. As a friend, I felt so helpless and worried. On hindsight, I knew that had I not picked up her call, there was a real chance that she could have seriously hurt herself—or done something even worse. I do not think I could have lived with myself had I not done something on my side to help. After an almost two hour call, I remember praying with her and making sure that she had calmed down before hanging up the phone.

This began the journey of walking beside my friend Paige and her mental health struggles. Every two months or so, she would share with me her down moments with depression. Her triggers were usually due to academic stress. As a fellow sister-in-Christ, I tried my best to encourage her whenever I could, though the time difference and physical distance meant I was not always able to get the latest updates. Thankfully, I knew that she had a Christian community supporting her and it comforted me to know that there were other people watching out for her.

But that changed in her final year of undergraduate studies. She was assaulted. To make matters worse, her assailant was from her Christian community. As a result of her attack, she developed Post Traumatic Stress Disorder (PTSD) on top of her depression. While she tried to seek solace at her church, her church took the side of the assailant—who was a leader at church— and blamed her for allowing the attack to occur. Not being able to get the support she needed, she walked away from that church.

When she shared about this incident with me, I thought that she had left *that* particular church community as she was understandably hurt by their response to her. However, when I spoke to her later about finding a Christian community to support her, she went into a tirade about Christians in general. She blamed her previous church, saying that their response possibly exacerbated her PTSD and made her unable to reconcile the character of God with the behaviour of Christians. Being on the receiving end, it felt painful as she labelled all Christians as hypocrites— even though she later clarified that I was not included in that category. Nevertheless, I knew that I needed to hear this from her to know how hurt she felt by the church.

As a cell group leader in my church currently, I make it a point to consider how our interaction with our members can inadvertently turn away people if we are not careful.

Do we as leaders sometimes further hurt our hurting or grieving members, when we do not put in enough effort to comprehend what they are going through? This is especially so for people struggling with mental health issues. Based on my friend's narrative, it sounded like the church leaders were more concerned with their own leader's reputation than with what actually happened.

Having said that, I am not in the position to assess the church's response as I have only heard Paige's side of the story. I believe that her church leaders and members had tried their best and had the best intentions in helping her but it simply came out the wrong way.

Having journeyed with my friend and her mental health struggles over these past five years, here's the key lesson I've learned.

To Be Present With Her
Like Job's friends who sat in silence with Job even as he suffered, this means being there for my friend through her rants, whether on the phone, online, or in person. While I could not always reply her immediately due to the time difference and circumstances, I always tried my best to reply her at some point. Whenever she returned to Singapore, I would meet with her for lunch; I once accompanied her to her psychiatrist appointment. As I am a healthcare professional, she would discuss her medications openly with me and ask me about her current treatments. I usually try my best to advise her about the side effects or address any concerns she has with her medication.

Over time, I have realised that it is not about the things I can say to bring her to a better state in mental health. It is simply about being there as a friend when she needs me the most. The passage from Ecclesiastes 4:9–12 has been a firm reminder to me about the importance of community and the need for me to be keep being that helpline to her.

> *Two are better than one,*
> *because they have a good return for their labour:*
> *If either of them falls down,*
> *one can help the other up.*
> *But pity anyone who falls*
> *and has no one to help them up.*
> *Also, if two lie down together, they will keep warm.*
> *But how can one keep warm alone?*
> *Though one may be overpowered,*
> *two can defend themselves.*
> *A cord of three strands is not quickly broken.*

My Friend is Still Struggling

If you are looking for a happy ending, this story does not have one. My friend is still out of church and is still dealing with PTSD and depression. Has my friend re-attempted suicide? Yes. Do I hope that I can reconcile her back to the Christian community? With God's help, I hope so. I believe that if she can find a loving and caring Christian community, she would be better able to cope with the stress she faces at work as well as her mental health condition.

She did share that she still believes in God and in what Christ has done. Her barrier to coming back to church however is the Christians who hurt her. She is fully aware of my Christian faith and while she says that our friendship has "nothing to do with religion", she's open to talking about Christianity. Right now, my prayer is that I can be a constant reflection of Christ's love to her so that she will eventually want to come back to a Christian community. Till then, I'm committed to just be a friend and available helpline to my friend.

*Chua JH**

A JOURNEY OF FINDING MORE QUESTIONS THAN ANSWERS

I first heard the news about my church friend's mental breakdown when I was overseas.

She was admitted to the Institute of Mental Health (IMH) after exhibiting disturbing behaviour in public, which led to her being arrested. The story only emerged after my friend's mother came to church on a Sunday morning, looking for her because she had not returned home the night before.

I can only imagine what it must have been like for my friend to have been held in police custody as well as in the IMH ward without her mother knowing initially. After my friend's discharge, I met up with her periodically and tried to encourage her with Scripture and messages to let her know I was praying for her. But even then, it was difficult to talk about her mental illness directly. I didn't know what the diagnosis was; I didn't know the details of her medication, including what the side effects were, although I knew that there certainly were side effects.

How do you walk alongside a friend when there's so little you know about their emotional and mental condition? How do you support them when the very topic of the mental illness is one which is so difficult to talk about in society and even in the Church? Moreover, it was clear that both her mental illness as well as the medication she was on affected her moods and personality, her thoughts and emotions; and this made our conversations challenging at times.

The stigma surrounding mental illness is certainly a very real issue. Somehow, we tend to still think that it is the patient's fault—for instance, thinking that they simply have a "weak mind" or constitution. Would we ever think that someone stricken with cancer was somehow to blame for his or her condition? And yet, when someone is undergoing depression, for instance, we throw words like "snap out of it" or "cheer up", hoping that it will be enough for them to recover. We find it hard to understand how someone could feel depressed or down, when they have much to be grateful for and there are other people in the world who have it worse than them. We avoid those with schizophrenia because we do not know how to relate to them, fearing the unpredictability of their behaviour, not daring to even look them in the eyes. It's often easier just to ignore the issue altogether.

Mental illness is something we don't understand and don't have the language to deal with. We find ourselves grasping for more meaningful words, other than "How are you feeling?" Do I try to help my friend look forward to the future, or bring up good memories from the past? If financial issues and caregiving concerns are on her mind, do I bring that up, given that these might be sensitive issues and provoke a certain response?

Since both of us are Christians, we prayed together but I somehow felt that there was more I could do to walk alongside her in this journey. At the same time, in sharing

Scripture with her, many of the Psalms seemed appropriate since they often spoke of cries for help and deliverance, and promises peace of mind, deliverance and protection. For example, Psalm 121:1–3 reads,

> *I lift up my eyes to the mountains—*
>   *where does my help come from?*
> *My help comes from the Lord,*
>   *the Maker of heaven and earth.*
> *He will not let your foot slip—*
>   *he who watches over you will not slumber;*

While holding on to these promises, I wrestled because whether physical or mental illness, we know that the Lord may not always grant full and complete healing.

How we think about mental illness, physical illness and healing relates to our theology, in terms of what we believe about God. As I have some background knowledge regarding mental health issues and have read up on psychological disorders such as schizophrenia, depression and anxiety, some of the theories I read about seem to point to the possibility that mental disorder can at times be the result of the interaction between biological predisposition and the stress caused by life experiences.

My friend's childhood wasn't easy. Her father passed away when she was relatively young. In school, she excelled, but she gave up what most would have thought to be a promising career in order to pursue her passion. As a result of that bold step, she incurred a rather large sum of debt. Being the sole breadwinner for her family definitely took a toll on her emotionally and mentally. From what I knew, her younger siblings had yet to find stable jobs, and were still heavily dependent on my friend for their needs. What does one need to know or be equipped with in order to walk with someone with mental illness? Do we need to know the exact diagnosis? Do we need to know how the different illnesses interact since they seem closely related? I knew my friend's illness affected her thought patterns and beliefs. She felt disturbed by voices she heard and believed that the police were surveilling her around where she lived and when she took the MRT. She made associations between her actions in terms of buying goods from certain stores and how that would affect the larger economy, and subsequently, firmly believed that her spending money would lead to some kind of disaster being averted. How was I to help her distinguish between what was real and what was not? Was it even my place to do so, or should I just be there for her, to listen to her when she wanted to share these thoughts with me?

Perhaps this is one of the key difficulties when walking alongside a friend who is going through mental illness. We don't quite know what to say or how to respond. If a close friend is going through a period of depression, where he/she may not wish to see anyone and have considerable difficulty getting through simple everyday activities, would we be able to just sit there and *be with* that friend? Or if my friend were to buy me an unnecessarily expensive gift from a certain store out of a sincere belief that it is good for the economy, how should I receive that gift? Do I simply accept it, reject it, or chide her for spending money on it and on me?

Due to the stigma and sensitivities surrounding this topic, it also seemed as if there was a great lack of communication between my friend's doctors and her family or friends.

Besides providing medication which might help stabilize moods or control hallucinations, should not the treatment processes be conducted in a more open format such that one's family and friends can be involved, and so that they know how to best support the patient?

After a few years, my friend seemed to be getting better. I followed up with her again, and this was when she told me that her mental illness was "in the past". She said that she was no longer in need of any treatment. However, the warning signs emerged again in the form of her social media posts, and I could tell that she was not doing so well in her career. Then she started posting our private messages on her social media, and after we met up, my friend even posted an audio recording of a conversation we had during one of our catch-up sessions—I was not aware that she was recording our conversation then. After that, some of our other friends started asking me questions, even those who did not know my friend. I did feel slightly wronged and maligned, because she had interpreted my text messages in a negative light, and her posting my private messages to her as well as the recorded conversation did feel like an invasion of privacy.

However, I was still more concerned about how to help my friend, as her condition seemed to be getting more and more serious. I did not confront my friend about her posts because I did not know how to bring up the topic and did not want to further aggravate the situation. Eventually however, my friend's mother finally spoke to me over the phone and asked me not to meet up with or contact my friend anymore, saying that I was aggravating her condition whenever we met up. Apparently, my friend would always feel inferior and her self-esteem would take a hit whenever we met, because the rest of us seemed to be doing so well in our respective lives compared to her.

At the time of writing this, I have no idea how my friend is coping. Her posts on social media seem to indicate that she is surviving, but it is likely that she does not recognize her need for help. The irony is that while social media helps us remain updated about each other's lives, it is also the very thing that makes us feel worse about ourselves, when we compare our lives to the lives of others which we see on social media.

Through this whole journey, I've walked away with more questions than answers. I wonder how the Church can be that body of support which walks alongside anyone who has mental health issues, and to work towards holistic care of the entire person—spiritual, physical and mental. Can we really be that open and authentic community that would devote time, attention and even money to help those who are going through periods of illness; to offer to attend appointments with them even? What can we do to turn our churches into spaces where all who come in would feel safe and welcomed despite their circumstances?

It is my hope that through greater awareness and increased conversation, we can move towards a better understanding of the issue of mental illness, and how we in the Church can better walk alongside those who are going through this journey.

Fern Leong

WE WILL ARISE AND SHINE

Sometime in mid-2014, my husband and I were invited by our church leaders to see a marriage counsellor because of an incident which took place during church camp where we had an argument that was witnessed by our cell members. We were informed that we would not be allowed to continue serving as cell group leaders unless we sought marriage counselling; our leaders seemed to think that our marriage was failing or facing serious issues. The response from our leaders is something that continues to affect me even till now.

Looking back, I can see how God assured us of this truth in His word:

> *And we know that all things work together for good to those who love God, to those who are the called according to* His *purpose.*
> *(Romans 8:28, NKJV)*

Whether or not we knew it then, Romans 8:28 was already at work in our lives.

And so, my husband and I complied—we scheduled meetings with our church marriage counsellor. At every meeting, my husband would struggle to contain his emotions and would often break down in tears. Looking back, my husband was having post-traumatic reactions, resulting in him having those emotional outbursts.

As we shared more, we were able to connect his responses to a particularly challenging time in late 2013, when my husband was a caregiver to his mom. She had taken ill suddenly and passed away in less than six months, on Good Friday. It was a very trying and traumatic time for him then.

As these episodes began to surface, our counsellor suggested that my husband should see a psychiatrist rather than a marriage counsellor. From his observation and interaction during our counselling sessions, our counsellor felt that my husband could be suffering from depression and that this could be the real issue, rather than our perceived 'marriage problems'. Indeed, when we finally saw a psychiatrist, my husband was diagnosed as having Post-Traumatic Stress Disorder (PTSD) causing Major Depressive Disorder (MDD), otherwise known as Clinical Depression.

I was totally shocked. Truth be told, I knew little about PTSD and depression. I had only heard of PTSD from movies about soldiers returning from war, and I was not able to reconcile this diagnosis of PTSD with the fact that we were living in Singapore where things are relatively calm and peaceful.

When my husband was first diagnosed, my feelings were dominated by fear and anxiety because my husband's mood had been dramatically affected even further by the knowledge of his mental illness. He would be sad and emotional, as well as very easily upset, with random outbursts where he would cry for a long period of time. I remember in particular, one incident when we were having dinner with our mentors. Without warning, my husband suddenly had a meltdown and I felt shocked, embarrassed and fearful. Thankfully, our mentors were calm, patient and caring throughout the episode and they allowed him to cry for almost 45 minutes without imposing any judgment or even attempting to stop him. At the same time, they were trying to keep us both calm with words of encouragement.

However, not everyone is as understanding, patient or willing to understand. Even amongst Christians, PTSD, depression or mental illness is not a topic we can freely discuss because of the stigma associated with mental illness. Even when we shared openly and honestly with those around us, many did not know what to do or how to have a meaningful conversation with us. Some would unleash well-meaning but harsh words against my husband —telling him that he is not healed because of his lack of faith, that he is wallowing in self-pity, and he should just 'snap out of it'.

In all honesty, I was one of those people. As time passed, things were not developing and I was getting more and more impatient with my husband. How was I supposed to deal with his emotional outbursts, sudden crying and even unwarranted accusations at times? His mental state definitely put our marriage to the test. Once, when I was at the end of my own rope, my husband's psychiatrist met with me to hear my frustrations as a spouse and caregiver, as well as to share specific coping strategies that I could adopt. What I needed then was sound, practical advice—advice on not letting or imposing significant decisions on my husband, or how not to be alarmed when he has a melt down, or even how to be conscious of speaking harshly to him and to try to be patient instead.

It was also during that period of testing that I turned in desperation to God. I cried for help and told God that I could not do it on my own. In His grace and mercy, I felt God giving me His promise that He would lift my husband out of the miry clay, He would turn our ashes to beauty and our mourning to dancing.

Still, for many years, the situation did not immediately improve, despite regular trips to the psychiatrist and various combinations of medication. My husband's relationship with God was also waning—he could not read the Bible and he struggled to worship God. Although we were both serving in the worship ministry, he stepped down from the ministry within four months of receiving his diagnosis due to his inability to connect and praise God. As for me, I recall weekends where I served in the worship ministry and looked down at my husband from the stage, only to see him unable to give his fullest worship.

He used to be such a joyful worshipper. Seeing him unable to sing and worship God really broke my heart. I knew that much as I would like to continue to serve in the worship ministry, I was unable to look at him and live with the knowledge that my husband was unable to do so. Sadly, that led me to step down from the ministry as well—a ministry that I so loved and enjoyed serving in.

Sometime in January 2015, when my husband was retrenched, I began to ask God to give me wisdom and strength to help my husband turn to the Word of God. I also decided to take active steps to help him with this. Each morning I would do a short devotion with my husband, have him read a short passage of Scripture and we would pray together. It was a struggle each day. Although

Walking with the Wounded

my husband used to be a very active person he became perpetually tired and exhausted because of the effect of his depression on him. Even taking short walks was a challenge. It was draining for me not just emotionally but also physically.

However, I pressed on and even thought of different ways I could lift his spirits, such as baking and cooking his favourite foods for him—we tried *everything we could think of* to spur on his healing and recovery. We even paid for a thorough healing session which seemed to help initially, but he relapsed almost immediately. This time, his dosage even had to be increased.

I had had enough. I was angry, frustrated and often caught myself slipping into a depressive state as well. Were these two tough years not enough? How much more was I expected to take? While I was patiently caring for him and looking out for him and his welfare, who was looking out for me?

During this difficult time, one of the prayers I had been constantly praying and seeking God about was whether my husband should take a break from work. I thought it would be good for him to take a break and enrol into Tung Ling Bible School (TLBS). I had gone through the course once, and it was such a good, refreshing experience for me. I felt that it would be an opportunity for him to find space to slow down and live at a more manageable pace.

A glimpse of hope came sometime in mid-2016, when we were once again at church camp. My husband was in a very bad state then as he was frustrated with himself at being unable to 'get better'. During the camp, he had an encounter with God where He sensed God leading him into reconciliation on certain issues in his life. It was then that He also felt prompted by God to take a sabbatical from work to enrol into TLBS for a three-month course in the School of Ministry. During those three months, I begin to see him feeling more energized, joyful and looking forward to a brand new day. It was still a slow healing process as his PTSD and depressive symptoms continued, such as vivid flashbacks that triggered meltdowns.

In December 2017, while on a trip to Israel with TLBS, my husband bravely shared his testimony on board a boat at the Sea of Galilee. During his sharing, I sensed the Spirit of God speak to me, telling me that we would both "Arise, shine" (Isaiah 60:1). I saw a picture of Jesus pulling a thick white rope up from a deep dark pit, and at the end of that rope was my husband being lifted out. I suddenly remembered the promise that I had heard from God some time back—that He would lift my husband out of the miry clay. It was a life-changing moment for us to receive this promise from God, and to know that He was with us despite the trying circumstances. It was also significant that my sister's family was with us in Israel and it was the first time they heard his testimony. Although he knew that they were aware of it and had been praying for him during this period, it was the first time that my husband had openly shared about it.

Since then, my husband's mental state of health miraculously began to heal. It was gradual, but with time, it became clear that God was leading my husband to rediscover God's love for him and his identity as a child before God. By May 2018, he was completely off his medication. In July 2018, we both enrolled into TLBS again, this time for the School of Leadership. I am thankful to God for giving us the opportunity of attending TLBS together as a couple. During the three months we both heard from God separately, about the ministry that He would like us to pursue together. It would be a ministry of supporting those who have mental health struggles—both them and their caregivers.

It has been a tough four-and-a-half-year struggle for my husband and I, but it has also drawn us closer to God and closer to each other. Our relationship was put to the test and has come forth purified.

It has also been a journey of God pruning me and cultivating patience, love and empathy in me. I would not have survived this journey without Jesus being my anchor of hope and also having caring and loving mentors who formed a community that journeyed with us without judgment or prescribing solutions. Instead, they prayed and encouraged us throughout the four and a half years and loved us as we were throughout the struggle. I am also grateful to family, friends, doctors and counsellors for their support; without which, it would have been a very tough and lonely journey.

Having been through this dark tunnel ourselves, my husband and I now hope to use our experience to help others. To journey with them and encourage those with mental illnesses, to share that there is a light at the end of the tunnel and not to despair because our God truly is a God of Hope. Despite our human weaknesses and struggles, in Him, we can truly *"Arise, shine"*.

Janet Chan-Lee

PERSPECTIVES FROM A WIFE

The year 2016 was supposed to be a celebratory year for us—Mike and I would be married for 20 years, a milestone for us as a couple. As it turned out however, the year would involve an episode in our lives that would cause us to question the marriage vows we had to each other.

What does it mean to love and hold someone, in sickness and in health?

Through this season, I came to discover my answer to this question in a very unforgettable manner.

It all started when Mike slowed down in his work during the first quarter of 2016 after an exceptionally busy year in 2015. When business was slow, he started to be in a state of panic. I remember the talks we had and that I had mentioned the possibility that he might be experiencing 'burn out'. Prior to this, since 2012, Mike had bouts of panic attacks in the night. He would then quickly recover from the episodes without us having to ever be suspicious of anything being wrong, and we therefore did not know he had a panic disorder. So we went on with our lives, without having to address this issue. I thought that Mike was better too as I did not see him waking up in the middle of the night or hear him complain of any chest tightness, which used to be the case.

Sometime in May 2016, when Mike and I both came down with a bout of flu, Mike began to complain about a loss of taste and smell after taking his medicine. I did not think much of it, assuming that it was probably the side-effects of his medicine. I told him to be patient and that his sense of taste and smell would return soon. I was so wrong. Mike started to become very paranoid about his condition and his panic attacks became more frequent. When I sensed that something was amiss, I began to observe him more closely. By then, it had been three weeks since he had lost his sense of taste and smell, and I too, started to feel very uneasy about the entire thing.

Our search for a cure brought us to various general practitioners (GPs), specialists like ENT doctors and even a neurologist. Finally, we turned to Traditional Chinese Medicine (TCM). We tried acupuncture, chiropractic and any other methods that Mike researched online that seemed to be helpful to restore his sense of taste and smell. We even tried alternative methods like the emotional freedom technique, which involved tapping on the various meridian points (energy hot spots) of the body to reduce cortisol levels and restore energy balance; as well as meditation which is supposed to help enable greater calmness and control over one's anxiety.

All these methods brought short-term 'recovery', but also much disappointment and frustration when Mike realised that there was no long-term improvement. During this time, his panic attacks had only gotten more frequent and intense. For a period of about five months, we were completely resistant to visiting a psychiatrist as we thought about the stigma involved and the consequences of having to take psychiatric medication.

I personally carried these reservations as I used to be a caregiver for my sister who took psychiatric medication for almost 13 years before finally losing the battle to bipolar disorder. It made me lose trust and have lots of misgivings for this particular path of treatment. We had several family discussions along with our son about Mike taking psychiatric medication. We continued to remain resistant until finally relenting in November 2016 because Mike was really not doing well. He was experiencing exceptionally dark thoughts; in his own words, he said that he was "lost in the woods, a very dense forest". We simply could not see the light at the end of the tunnel and we felt really lost and stuck in that season.

With the help of my sister-in-law and some friends, we found an extremely competent and reliable psychiatrist. That was when we started the journey of recovery for Mike. As it turned out, I eventually discovered that the psychiatrist was the *same* psychiatrist who first treated my sister (with very good results) before she switched psychiatrists due to unforeseen circumstances. What a full circle we had come to!

We hope that some of the lessons learnt during these dark times and challenging season of our lives will continue to be an encouragement to both patients and caregivers alike, so that they know there is light at the end of the tunnel even while they take practical steps to keep moving ahead.

• ***Find the most appropriate treatment quickly & early.***
After the first two-hour consultation with the psychiatrist, Mike was officially diagnosed to have panic or anxiety disorder. Finally, the puzzle pieces of our life fell into place

and made sense as we examined his years of panic attacks prior to this diagnosis. Due to our lack of understanding, we simply ignored the 'tell-tale signs' of his illness. It then festered to become quite a monster for us to tame. On hindsight, I realised the importance of seeking reliable medical counsel and medical treatment as soon as possible. This is especially so in the cases of mental illness. Procrastination, avoidance or simply 'hoping' (without active steps) will not make the issue go away. The root cause of the illness must be dealt with.

- *Have faith and do your best to remain positive.*

As a Christian couple that had been married for 20 years at that time, I had never seen Mike in such a desolate state even though we had weathered through a number of crises together. He was just so broken down by his illness. I found it hard to recognise the man whom I married 20 years ago; he had become so fragile, timid, and needed a lot of care and attention. My sleep cycle and daily routines were disturbed, my work schedule was disrupted with lots of visits for the various treatments he was undergoing. I had no social life as I had to cancel my commitments to stay with Mike, just so that I would not lose him. I asked Jesus fervently, praying and hoping to get answers to my burning questions: "Would Mike be healed?", "Why us?", "How long more?". I heard no other words in response, except these two simple words: "Just walk".

And that was what we did. I trusted God and clung on tightly to my hope in God—the one who brought us together would heal Mike eventually. I would just walk and continue to count my blessings daily. Slowly and steadily, we saw slight improvements in Mike's condition. His panic attacks gradually became less frequent and intense, his sense of taste slowly returned and finally, he could smell the faintest scent—fresh bedsheets! During these times, I became so acutely aware of my helplessness and God's omnipotence. I was reminded to walk by faith and not by sight, trusting in God's timing to restore Mike's sense of taste and smell.

• ***Find a community/support group & practice self-care.*** Through this experience, I learnt the paramount importance of having a community of loved ones and friends who can render support during tough times. We did not want to share about Mike's condition with anyone until he was comfortable to. Once we did, support and help started to pour in and this provided great respite for me as his primary caregiver. I needed the occasional breaks so that I could have some self-care routines such as meeting up with my good friends over a meal, finding a listening ear for myself or simply designating some time to myself to process all that was going on. We should never feel embarrassed or shy to acknowledge our needs, or to ensure that we are being cared for so that we can walk the long journey ahead with our loved ones.

It has been more than two and a half years since Mike's recovery.

I am keenly aware that this season has made an indelible mark in our lives. We live with the fact that Mike's anxiety disorder may never be fully eradicated, but we can help manage it to prevent any exacerbation. We live with the 'new normal' and continue to make sure to take care of our own mental health. Mike has also learnt to carve out 'me' time and take care of his health more actively. As a family, we have taken time to connect more and also take trips together.

It is never an easy road to tread but with God's strength and help, I can finally say (quoting Mike): "We are finally out of the woods."

Wong Moy Yin

NB: Read Mike's story on page 1 and their son, Myer Wong's story on page 78.

SHARING THE JOURNEY

– Reflection –

When we speak of "walking with the wounded", we often find our attention drawn towards what is most obvious—the wound. We immediately respond in the ways we know best; we tend to the wound, dress it, and find ways to bring about complete and long-lasting healing.

But as the stories in this part of the book reveal to us, there is hardly any guarantee of full and complete healing as we continue on this journey. Yet the wounds that surface in us and in our loved ones cannot be ignored in some kind of quiet hope that they will somehow go away.

This poses a specific challenge to those who battle mental illness and their caregivers alike, because some wounds aren't always immediately obvious or discernible; what is seen in the external is hardly an accurate or clear representation of what might be happening on the inside. Myer put it beautifully in his story: we typically know what to do when someone falls, but in some moments of life, "[t]here are no wounds for you to help dress; it is a battle that [the wounded] alone must fight."

For caregivers, this tension is a particularly perilous space to navigate—*What is going on? And, what exactly am I expected do in this situation?* What begins as an earnest desire to help and to provide answers, gradually morphs into a state of helplessness that surfaces more questions than answers. As Sophie shares, "So here I am. Sensing the meaninglessness of trying to help others and knowing I can't really help myself sometimes."

What we learn from these caregivers through their stories, is that it is okay not to know or to have all the answers. It is okay not to know when things will start to look up. It is okay not to know what to say when your mentally ill parent, spouse or friend says: "What is this? What is happening to me?" It is okay to acknowledge your own needs, dependencies and weaknesses; even in the face of a wounded soul's dependence on you. As Moy Yin shares with us, self-care is all the more critical when we ourselves are giving care to others.

Through the stories, we come to realise that inasmuch as it may be an "entirely new experience" for those with mental illness, so it is for those providing care to them. When I picture Myer's description of his father's grappling with mental illness as being "like a child that's fallen down for the first time", I quickly realise that somewhere in that picture, there is a parent who is witnessing his/her child falling down "for the first time". That, too, is a new experience in itself and we need time to learn how to navigate it. Indeed, it is no different for us who give care to those who give care.

Perhaps, it all comes down to this—the "walking with" and the journeying alongside. It leads us to ponder and receive the God-given gift of companionship and community; to contemplate fundamental realities and questions such as: *Where are we going? Who are we going with?*

Are we heading in the same direction? What pace are we moving at? Whose pace are we moving to? When will we get there?

I think of Alice's story and how she came to know God through the obedience of her mother, who despite her psychosis, found herself somehow empowered to listen and obey the voice of God. *Are we heading in the same direction?* I am reminded of Janet and Moy Yin who sought to hold fast to their marriage vows in the face of "dark and challenging seasons" that have no clear view in sight: *Where are we going? Are we going there together?*

Through these stories, I've learnt that walking in the context of family and community means that we move to the pace of the slowest one amongst us. While with good intentions we may seek to pull others to our level and our pace, we must understand that they are not always capable of doing so ("we throw words like 'snap out of it' or 'cheer up', hoping that these will be enough motivation for them to recover").

As I continue to make sense of what I've read in these stories, I find myself somewhat assured by Moy Yin's sharing that in the midst of these burning questions, we may find the tender, loving voice of Jesus saying: "Just walk". Putting it all together, this must mean that we learn to walk to the pace of "the wounded"—whether the wounds are borne by those with mental illness *or* their caregivers, spouses, families and friends.

And as we do that for each other in the Gospel community, I am quickly understanding that this is how God reveals His heart for us and His ways towards us all—that His greatest assurance is not that He will *take away* our struggle, pain or suffering; but that He will *be with us*. Perhaps, this is the *deepest* cry of all our hearts, that beyond the desire for restoration and healing, we want to know that someone will be *with us* and *stand by us*. As Jesus said to Peter, James and John in the garden of Gethsemane, "*My soul is deeply grieved, so that I am almost dying of sorrow. Stay here and stay awake and keep watch with Me*" (Matthew 26:38, AMP). The cry is one of companionship.

Psalm 23 reminds us of God's constant assurance that He is *with us* in the valley; He sets up a table and dines with us in midst of the storm, in the face of hidden and/or apparent monsters, and in our pain. As we learn how to *walk with* the wounded, we quickly come to see a measure of our own woundedness and discover how God is walking *with us* too, as caregivers to those with mental illness and even as caregivers *to the caregivers*. This is Gospel.

And while we may not be able to fight those battles for the wounded even as we stand *with* them, our continued presence might just be the very thing they need to go one step further. In this, our anthem as caregivers is not unlike that of Samwise Gamgee in J. R. R. Tolkien's *The Lord of the Rings*: "I can't carry it for you, but I can carry you."

The truth is that most of these stories present no triumphant resolution or clear conclusion. As a woven tapestry of shared experiences, we learn that we—the wounded, the caregivers, the enveloping community—can only just keep walking. And as all these stories bear hint of, as long as we choose to journey together and point our hearts in the right direction, we will get to where we are supposed to be—*Home*—no matter how long the journey takes.

And all I know is that I still don't know a lot
I don't know how it ends
I'm in the middle of this plot
I found grace for the man that I am not
I found out the day I lost myself
Was the day that I found God

(The Day That I Found God, Switchfoot)

Jonathan Cho
Covenant Chambers LLC

SECTION 3 — WALKING TOWARDS THE LIGHT

SOUL CARE AS SPIRITUAL PRACTICE

There are happy people and there are sad people. I identify with the latter.

I remember struggling to be happy as a young boy. I had a fantastic childhood, a great family and had most of what I wanted as a child; but I struggled nevertheless. I struggled to smile in family pictures, to enjoy vacations and to have fun. I would say that the traits of sadness and melancholy would best describe my personality as a child.

As I grew older, I began noticing that this sadness and melancholy evolved into something entirely different. I started becoming really critical of myself—a perfectionist in every sense of the word. I was constantly concerned with how I was performing and what others thought of me. This paved the way to me becoming someone who was driven, deeply obsessed about performance and yet at the same time, deeply insecure and anxious.

Everything came to a head when I began to feel that there was something wrong with my body. At that point, I was sleeping anywhere between three to four hours a night, for the most part adopting a sedentary lifestyle and not being mindful of what and when I was eating. There were occasions when I was shaken out of my sleep, my heart racing, body drenched in sweat and the whole world seemingly spinning out of control.

Realising that something might be wrong with my body, I went for a blood test. A few days later, I received results that were unfavourable to say the least.

All this happened six months into my new appointment as Lead Pastor of a church.

I remember the exact moment when I received news of my diagnosis. My wife received a call from our doctor while I was preaching in my church. I was in the middle of a series on miracles and my sermon title for that week was "Dealing with Unanswered Prayer".

As I wrapped up my message on how we can walk through the disappointments, sufferings and pain of life with absolute trust and faith in God, my wife broke the news to me. I wish I could say that in that moment, I was filled with faith and courage. But the truth is that I was extremely fearful.

My initial thoughts were, "I am going to die young. I have disqualified myself from my ministry. God has abandoned me. I am going to be a burden to my wife. I should die."

The morning after the diagnosis, I was home alone. I toyed with the idea of suicide for a long time. On hindsight, it was completely irrational for me to come to such a conclusion, however, in that moment, it felt like the most logical and right thing to do.

Feelings of deep shame, insecurity, sadness and anger all came at the same time. I was overwhelmed by the deluge of emotions which was followed swiftly by an onslaught of lies.

I decided after a prolonged battle that I needed to distract myself. So I turned to the mind-numbing world of social media. As I opened the app, the first article that came up was about a young lead pastor, who after an extended battle with depression, panic attacks and suicidal thoughts; had taken his own life in his church office.

He left behind his wife and three boys.

After reading the article, I began to weep and was immediately shaken out of the emotional swirl I had allowed myself to be pulled into. I thought to myself that this could very well be me, this could be my wife, and that I must never let this happen. It was then that I decided that it was time to fight.

A Hard Battle

I am happy to say that as I write, I have lost 15 kilograms, received positive test results and have made significant progress in managing my emotional health. All of that came at the end of what I would describe as a long arduous process.

I grew up in a persuasion that firmly believes that God is able to perform miracles, breakthroughs and victories in a moment. In many ways, I still hold on to that belief. But my healing journey was one that involved hard work, perseverance, discipline and patience.

My wife was a great help, support and motivator in my journey. Aside from that, I saw the contrast between the life that I was experiencing and the promises of Scripture, and it left me deeply discontented. I was pastoring a church, reading Scripture, worshipping and doing all the things one should do as a Christian. Yet, I was mentally drained and emotionally broken.

I desperately wanted to see the words of Jesus in the gospel of Matthew—which says that He gives us "rest for our souls"—made a reality in my own life. I was anxious, over-busy and exhausted. These were all traits that were contrary to Jesus' vision of rest.

I chanced upon Eugene Peterson's paraphrase of that passage which suggests that the way to experience that rest was for us to adopt Jesus' way of living and "learn the unforced rhythms of grace".

Pastor and speaker John Mark Comer worded it beautifully when he said, "If you want to experience the life of Jesus, you have to adopt the lifestyle of Jesus."

By lifestyle, he meant the rhythms, rituals, routines and practices of one's life.

I sought to develop certain practices for my life by drawing inspiration from the life of Jesus in the gospels, early church fathers, as well as godly people I admired. Here are a couple that I have put into practice.

1. Slowing Down
As a culture, we have a bias towards hurrying. Ours is a culture that values speed, efficiency and quickness.

Philosopher and theologian Dallas Willard is famous for saying, "Hurry is the great enemy of spiritual life in our day. You must ruthlessly eliminate hurry from your life."

In many ways, I am sure we can all relate to that. For me, I realised that I was restless because I had adopted a pace of life that did not permit me to abide with God. I had no margin, headspace nor moment where I was unhurried, to simply rest.

Learning to slow down was essential to overcoming anxiety and stress. It is a practice that goes against the grain of our culture but paramount for the well-being of our soul and mind.

2. Sabbath

Sabbath is an ancient idea and practice of intentional rest that has long been discarded by much of the Church and our world. Sabbath is by no means a new concept, but it has largely been forgotten by the modern church.

There are many debates among Christians on the exact day on which we ought to sabbath. I simply practise a full day of intentional rest, delight and worship unto God. And for me, that happens on Monday.

On Mondays, I turn off my text notifications, I stay off work and news that worry me, I read from a Bible that isn't my regular preaching Bible, and I rest and spend time nourishing my soul. These practices, though seemingly insignificant, have saved my life. Sabbath is something that I look forward to each week. It is when I meet God and myself. I firmly believe that this is a rhythm that humanity was designed to live with—to work and to rest.

Pastors and Emotional Health

What was particularly haunting about the article on the pastor's suicide, which I mentioned earlier, were the words his wife said to their church just days before he took his life.

She said, "We still have a long way to go to work through it, but we are all in. You guys, he loves this place so much. He didn't want to stop. He would have kept on going and going and going and it probably would have cost him his life. That's how much he loves all of you, that's how much he loves this place."

Tragically, it did cost him his life.

As a pastor, this tragic story left me with a couple of thoughts. The first is that pastors, in their desire to serve God and people well, can so easily do so at the expense of their own health and well-being. Another thought would be that pastors, though deeply spiritual and heavily involved in spiritual activity, are not immune to emotional and mental brokenness.

As a church, we have begun to teach extensively on developing such practices for life and the need to pursue emotional health. We have committed to doing a series at the start of each year with an emphasis on the mind, soul and internal world. A fruit of these teachings is a real openness in my community to share openly about struggles with emotions, insecurity and mental well-being. A common realization for many who felt stuck in their spirituality was that as they began to pursue emotional health, they felt a progression in their spiritual life.

I think author Pete Scazzero sums it all up brilliantly with his magnum opus of a line that goes, "Emotional health and spiritual maturity are inseparable. It is not possible to be spiritually mature while remaining emotionally immature."

My hope is that as pastors, church leaders and Christians in general; we will begin to realise that emotional health is not distinct and separate from our goal of spiritual maturity. If we want to experience the promise of Scripture, of life in all its fullness, then we must be whole in body, soul and spirit.

Andre Tan
Pastor
The City Singapore

A PASTOR'S CONFESSION: PRESS THE "PAUSE" BUTTON

In 2010, a call changed my perspective forever.

"Colin Tan committed suicide!" He was a youth leader in my previous church. Someone dear to both my wife and I. We were shocked to the core. Many questions and thoughts flooded our minds. But we had no answers.

Yet, we knew we had to move on. We refused to be victims of grief. By His grace, we wanted to turn this messy emotional experience into His mighty message for all.

With my wife's blessing, I embarked on a book project with a few friends to study and understand the impact of depression among young people. This book *My Voice: Overcoming* was published in 2011.

Eight years on the mental health situation has not improved very much. Suicide figures are still high amongst the young. Depression and anxiety are hitting our young fiercely and relentlessly. The advent of smart phone does not help the situation.

Press the "Pause" Button
"I left XXX church because they ignored me and my condition."

"I was hurt because they blamed me for seeing a doctor."

"I was labelled as faithless and attention-seeking because of my meltdown."

The list goes on.

I've heard such remarks too often in my last 10 years of listening to and journeying with those who came to see me. Dealing with common misconceptions about mental health is already tough. Dealing with misconceptions about mental health in the faith arena is even tougher. While some faith convictions among church leaders are very admirable, some border on heresy and some are plain wrong.

There have been moments I was so angered by the wrong advice given or statement made to those suffering with depression that I was tempted to call the Christian leaders to "scold" them.

But grace came through for me because I realised I had been there before. If not for the research I had done for my book, I would be just as guilty as many of them. Hence, I now focus my energy towards building bridges with pastors and connecting them to mental health knowledge.

The best way to deal with stigma and misconception is with right medical knowledge. And I believe that is why the Lord is redirecting my attention to equipping the Church. The Body of Christ is His redemptive agent in this world of need. And with the Body of Christ properly equipped, we

Walking Towards the Light

could provide the caring community with the right skills and knowledge to journey with more people.

Press the "Pause" Button
In 2017, a call came.

During my devotion, I felt a strong witness within my spirit that God wanted me to bring the message on mental health to His Church. I initially struggled with this.

Firstly, the message on mental health is a universal message. More people needed to know and be equipped to handle this. Why just to the Church?

Secondly, I was apprehensive of how some churches with certain theological persuasions would receive such a message. To them, mental health issues were primarily an issue of demonization. "Just cast the demons out. Problem solved."

Yet, as I meditated more on the call, I realised the sacredness of the call.

I remembered my mentor's perspective: The world is in need because the Church is in trouble.

Having been a pastor for more than 27 years, I find that an average pastor does not have enough knowledge about mental health to know the difference between sadness and depression. Most pastors would either chide or correct the person for a lack of faith. Or some would care for the person but inadequately because of the lack of knowledge.

Some extreme cases could even lead to further breakdown or worse, loss of life. R was suffering from bipolar disorder. Her treatment prevented her from conceiving. A faith speaker came to her church and spoke against medication. "By faith", she stopped her medicine. And she conceived twins almost immediately! Towards the end of the first trimester, her depressive moods came back. She could not cope without medication so she resumed her medication and lost both children through a miscarriage.

Could this tragedy have been prevented? I don't know.

R's situation, of hearing a faith healer or speaker calling Christians to stop taking medicine, is not uncommon. There is a stream of Christianity that does not approve of medication for mental health conditions. To them, taking medicine displays a lack of faith. Yet they have no problem with Panadol or any medication for headaches. We need to understand that mental brokenness requires either medical treatment, or a spiritual response or both. We need to discern in each case what is appropriate.

There are a lot of common misconceptions about mental health conditions and medication. You can check out my book for some of them.

Press the "Pause" Button

I am very thankful for my senior pastor who is supportive of my calling to address mental health issues. He allowed me to begin the education process with the pastoral team.

We brought in psychiatrists and occupational therapists to conduct a mental health seminar with our pastoral team. They spent two full days learning about the various types of mental health conditions and the appropriate immediate responses to them. We also spent time studying Scripture to ensure that we are aligned to biblical worldviews too.

Twice a year, we organise mental health related talks for those who are interested in the church. From dementia to anxiety. From caregivers to curious individuals. From an hour's talk to an almost full-day seminar. We organise them to cater to the diverse interests and needs of the church.

We also weave in mental health issues and stories into our weekend sermons.

Currently, we are initiating support groups for people with mental health conditions and their caregivers. We host monthly prayer meetings for people involved in this arena. And we are also in talks with psychiatrists and counsellors to audit our in-house education and equipping programmes to raise our competency in managing mental health issues among our flock.

In the near future, we hope to share what we have learnt with other pastors and churches in Singapore so that together, we can arise as the healing community of Christ for the hurting and mentally wounded souls.

Press the "Pause" Button
The work with those suffering with mental health issues is not over. We have barely started. And in the process, I realised a huge need for us to learn to listen again. We Singaporeans are moving way too fast for our good. No wonder some call us 'rush-ians'.

There is a need for us to learn to PAUSE.

Take a deep breath.

Stay in the moment.

Let the world pass you by.

Focus on the person in front of you. And LISTEN.

But many of us cannot do this very well, myself included.

Press the "Pause" button.

If you are still reading this, you have indeed pressed the "Pause" button over the other demands of your life. Thank you for reading my confession. I owe you a debt for "hearing" me out. A debt of love.

> *Owe nothing to anyone except to love one another; for he who loves his neighbor has fulfilled the law. For this, "You shall not commit adultery, You shall not murder, You shall not steal, You shall not covet," and if there is any other commandment, it is summed up in this saying, "You shall love your neighbor as yourself." Love does no wrong to a neighbor; therefore love is the fulfillment of the law. (Romans 13:8–10, NASB)*

And this is what we all need to do for those who are unwell among us. Love them. Love is best expressed through spending time listening to them.

Reflection

Before we attempt great campaigns or projects or seminars, we need to first learn to listen to our own soul. Pressing the "Pause" button is good for our soul.

How are you doing today?
How are you connecting with God in your soul today?
What can you do to tend to the Holy Temple within you?

Please take care of yourself. Then can you be ready to take care of others.

In closing, I would like to share this simple reflective poem for your soul.

> *You can't be kind if you are not here.*
> *You can't be loving if you are not here.*
> *You can't be patient if you are not here.*
>
> *For you to be here, you need to press the pause button.*
> *To stop texting.*
> *To stop thinking about your next agenda.*
> *To stop for a moment.*
>
> *Be here.*
> *Listen.*
> *Feel.*
> *Love.*
> *Understand.*
> *Then, your world will change.*

Chua Seng Lee
Deputy Senior Pastor
Bethesda Bedok-Tampines Church

MY TEN BLACK YEARS

The Onset of Depression
The day my clinical depression ambushed me, I was preaching at a friend's ordination service. Because of my divorce I couldn't be part of his ordination council, but he wanted very much for me to be involved so he had me speak at his ordination service. After the service I was to go join a young adults evangelistic camp. I had to pick up a friend and then go to the camp site. But as I left the ordination service, it was as though somebody turned off all my switches. I felt I was walking in water. Simple movements took great effort. I had no strength and no heart for anything.

The evangelistic camp was a disaster. They had asked me to be involved because I enjoyed interacting with people in person and from the pulpit. But most of the camp, I was hiding in my room. I didn't want to see anybody. The only relief I got was to take hot showers so most of the time I was in the bathroom under the shower. I dragged myself out to do my talks then quickly retreated under the shower.

Seeking Help in My Pain
I was in horrendous emotional pain and so I sought out a psychiatrist. He worshipped at the evening service of my church and someone recommended him. I told him my story and he said he was not surprised that I was in depression because I had gone through multiple losses,

one after another. Among my losses: I had lost one wife to cancer, another to marital breakdown. Because of my marital breakdown I had lost my reputation and most of my ministry. And I was raising two children on my own. The psychiatrist started me on antidepressants and saw me once a week for counselling. He said that I should be over the worst of it in six months. It would be six of some of the worst months in my life. (The months leading up to my first wife's death from cancer were very hard too.)

I recall lying on the sofa every day; no strength and no will to do anything. The 1998 World Cup was on and I could not enjoy watching it, which should give you a clue as to how bad a shape I was in since I am a football fan. I was a single parent so I had to force myself to do grocery shopping for the family. (We had a helper who did the cooking.) I would go to bed around 11 p.m. every night, wake up around 1 a.m. and not be able to sleep again. It was horrible lying in the dark waiting for the dawn. The emotional pain was so bad that I toyed with the idea of suicide. But I quickly pushed the idea aside when I thought of my two sons. Their mother had died and the second marriage had broken up. They had no parent except me. It would be horribly irresponsible if I checked out too.

I was in constant contact with my friend and counsellor, the late Anthony Yeo. (I was in Petaling Jaya then and he was in Singapore.) We communicated mainly by email. And in the early days, I called my psychiatrist every day. I know he had patients but he would give me some time and listen to my pain whenever I called. Face-to-face visits then were once a week. He said I would be over the worst of it in six months, but life is lived one day at a time. Six months took forever to come.

I was grateful that the ministry I worked with, the Graduates Christian Fellowship of Malaysia gave me whatever time off I needed. But I also felt very guilty about not being able to carry out my regular duties. My two concerns: take care of my two boys, and recover from the depression—though I was not sure if I would ever get over it. Responses from the Christian community were mixed. Some stayed away because they really didn't know how to deal with someone with depression. There would be those who wanted me to snap out of it or some spiritual equivalent of snapping out of it like "if you prayed hard enough…".

What Didn't Help
I wasn't surprised that the church often didn't know what to do when their members, especially when their leaders suffer from complex brokenness. When I told some of my leaders that I needed time to recover from my grief when my first wife died, some said that I had the responsibility to get back on my saddle as soon as possible. They said that if the CEO of a major company were to let his staff know that he was wounded it would affect the morale of the company. I said I wasn't a CEO. I was a brother and I was hurting badly, but I don't think they understood. If I was just a layman I think I would have received more sympathy. But Christians put their leaders on pedestals. Leaders are not meant to fail or to be wounded. Or be depressed. I would like to think that the situation is better today.

Lots of people gave me all sorts of suggestions as to how I could get over my depression. I know they cared and were well meaning. But often I would feel that by asking me to get over my depression, they did not accept me in my pain. In caring for someone, we need to accept them as they are before we help them to get to where they should be. By "rushing me to get well" they seemed to be telling me that they did not accept me as I was, the first step in any healing journey. Perhaps it pained them to see me in my pain and their desire to see me healed was as much a desire for them to get over their discomfort as it was for my healing.

What Helped
Those who were most helpful to me were those who listened and who didn't give too much advice. They were just there with me. And they were there for me. They helped take my sons to church services, to tuition, to football games, to the movies, to taekwondo grading, etc. They were just there.

Kudos too to my sons who had to live with a dad who was lying on the sofa most of the day. They needed and deserved a dad who was more involved in their lives. I pray the Lord will recompense them in this life or the next.

Above all, I thank God for Anthony Yeo my friend and counsellor, and for my psychiatrist. He used antidepressants judiciously to help balance my brain biochemistry, but it was the long hours of loving wise conversations that were key to my healing. And then there were the many who prayed for me. God heard. God was merciful.

Leaving the Valley
My psychiatrist was right. I did get over the worst of my depression in six months. But I needed another year or two to regain any sense of full normalcy. And more time beyond that to regain the joy and shalom I now experience.

God's gift of Bernice as my wife was a key factor in my healing. Even now I am on alert for any signs of impending depression. When they appear, I do what I need to do to nip them in the bud. I now have a psychiatrist in Singapore, a dear friend whom I see every four months or so, more for spiritual friendship than for therapy. I do what I need to do for my mental, emotional and spiritual health.

Paul tells us that whatever help we receive in our time of brokenness enables us to help others in turn (2 Corinthians 1:3–4). I think I would be a much poorer people-helper and mentor if I had not gone through my experience of depression. It was a humbling experience that taught me the fragility of life and our need for God. My motto now is "life is hard, but God is real".

The God of Grace
I also found out much later that the Lord was working through me even in my depression. Remember that young adult evangelistic camp when my depression first emerged? I learnt much later that someone chose to be a follower of Jesus in response to one of my talks. And someone wrote the following about a mentoring group I ran while I was depressed:

> *... halfway through the year, I stepped into your home. I was shocked by your haggard appearance. You were lying on the couch. Depressed. On Lithium. (I was on Sertraline.) Muttering about the sadness and the melancholy of Rivendell and Lothlorien. You told us: "If you think I'm not fit to mentor you, I totally understand. You don't have to come back for future sessions." We saw you at your lowest.*

Your life was in pieces. And even then you still loved Jesus and you still loved us. So we came back. That was the most powerful small group I've been in.

Truly God's power is made perfect in weakness.

Tan Soo-Inn
Chairman
Graceworks Private Limited

DISCERNMENT TO HEAL

Is Discernment so Difficult?
I remember, as a church leader during my National Service days, learning about healing through Reinhard Bonnke's crusades and John Wimber's healing ministry. I wanted to bring healing to people with physical symptoms and illnesses. I found it difficult to know how to counsel church members when praying for healing, I was not sure when to ask them to wait for healing and when it was better not to wait and seek medical help immediately. Then things got more confusing as the question of spirit involvement came into the picture.

Here are four conflicting incidents which have shaped my view about discernment and healing:

1. A church worship leader Misha (not her real name) was secretly nursing depression and those counselling her had become exhausted and discouraged. We identified two primary factors that contributed to her condition: a) her resentment towards her mother; and b) her low self-esteem. We approached her mother, who reluctantly revealed that Misha was an unwanted pregnancy. Without mentioning this to Misha, we prayed over her and as we did so, she fell to the floor, took a foetal position and started to cry uncontrollably. From that time, she started to recover and sensed the Lord leading her into child evangelism work. She has now served in that ministry for over 10 years.

2. This is about a family who had been involved in Thai Buddhism. The father was an altar boy at the temple. The family became Christians and started to attend my church. However, their seven-year-old daughter was disruptive at services, standing up, shouting and climbing over the pews. It seemed like she was hyperactive (maybe with ADHD) and ill-disciplined. Her parents eventually brought her to the front for prayer one day and she could not be held down by four men. Later, a few church leaders and I found out that she had a 'third eye' and was able to see spirits (e.g. those who had died at their place of tragedy in her neighbourhood). We spent a few weeks counselling, teaching and ministering to her. It culminated in a final encounter where she herself gave us words of discernment which led to her release. Her transformation was remarkable. She would wake up early to get her parents to church and was the best-behaved child, fully devoted to Jesus.

3. A young lady in her thirties who had been diagnosed with psychosis and depression had been stalking our church pastor since his previous church assignment. She had a fixation and obsession over him. She would often disrupt church services and constantly appear at the door of his house. Many of the church leaders and members saw her as a tool of the devil and prayed to contain her disruptive behaviours. I did as well. However, one day, we heard that she had taken her life and the sense of guilt that followed was overwhelming.

4. While I was directing a drug rehabilitation centre for ex-offenders, we once took in ex-offenders with diagnosed mental illnesses. There was an ex-prisoner we accepted into our halfway house who was an

NUS engineering graduate diagnosed with schizophrenia. He had killed his five-year-old nephew while playing with him, unprovoked. He seemed very quiet and was taking a high level of psychiatric medicine, but he could function in our programme. Eventually he was assigned to work at the thrift shop. He would also attend daily devotions. He even told some of us that "these last six months were the happiest days of my life". But one day he disappeared from the halfway house. We searched for two days, only to find out that he had gone to a HDB block adjacent to his nephew's block and jumped. We conducted the funeral with worship songs, decked in our best clothes to honour him before the Lord. Many of the residents had to go through counselling, wondering if they had inadvertently triggered his death with their actions and interactions with him or lack thereof. However, we discovered that he was intent on ending his life. He had carefully planned it and had also purchased a street directory a few days prior to his suicide to work out the route.

These contrasting stories leave me baffled on how to help Christians navigate mental health issues. Is there a biblical approach to guide us?

Insights from My Life Journey

Along my life journey, I've gathered certain insights into this question which are personal to me. I have found a theological basis for most of these insights. However, it is best to interpret them as one person's attempt at simplifying the complex issues surrounding how a gospel community can impact those with mental health issues.

I should first mention certain seasons of my life which have impacted how I came upon the insights I will share further below:

1. In my late teens and early twenties, I was part of the church team that prayed for healing for church members, including matters involving spiritual manifestations and spiritual oppression.

2. In my mid-twenties to late forties, I served for about 20 years with Wycliffe Bible Translators in Papua New Guinea[1] among two remote mountain tribal groups that practised spiritism and sorcery, and I witnessed God move to heal and bring revival among them.

3. In my late forties to early fifties, I served as a pastor, and also at a drug rehabilitation centre.

4. From my early fifties until now, I am the Managing Director of a Christian values-based psychiatric and psychological private practice called Promises (*www.promises.com.sg*).

With that background, here are some of my insights.

Why Should We Treat Mental Illness Any Differently?

- God's healing is for all dimensions of life, i.e. mental, physical, emotional and spiritual.

---

[1] While in Singapore people are often cautious to attribute mental health issues to the demonic, in Papuan communities that are involved in spiritism, over-spiritualisation is an issue and people will often attribute most ailments to spirits. They also easily submit their bodies and emotions to the control of spirits and tend to overreact, even if it is the Holy Spirit moving among them.

- The focus of prayer should simply be for wholeness and restoration.
- Prayer should include physical restoration, mental well-being, emotional regulation and spiritual freedom, regardless of whether it is a physical, mental, emotional or spiritual issue. Usually all factors are involved to some degree.
- Urgency in seeking professional help is just as critical for mental health issues as for physical health problems.
- The intent, urgency and openness on how physical ailments are approached and treated should also be applied for mental disorders regardless of the associated stigma.
- A wrong diagnosis can be disastrous. Often, diagnosing mental disorders is harder than for physical ailments.

Discernment Requires Multiple Approaches

- Discernment on how to pray should be sought for physical restoration, mental well-being, emotional regulation and spiritual freedom; regardless of whether it is a physical, mental, emotional or spiritual issue. Often, all factors are involved to some degree.
- Discernment of root issues will only help us know the order of approach, but all dimensions must be addressed through prayer and counsel.
- To attribute illness merely to demonic activity can shake a person's self-worth and assurance of salvation.
- Professional assessment should be taken into consideration.
- Professional psychiatric treatment is not outside of the grace of God, just as medical doctors and hospital treatment is God's grace given to all for our healing.

- Discernment which leads to professional psychiatric help does not mean it compromises our trust in the Lord because more likely than not, it will help us to pray with more precision.

Is Medication More Harmful than Helpful?
- Medicine is necessary to reduce the effect of symptoms so our natural system can cope better (similar to using antibiotics).
- Using medication does not mean it cannot be reduced or removed later.
- There are instances when medication has to be continued (similar to diabetic programs).
- Psychiatric medication often takes days to take effect. Professional advice should guide us in this regard.
- Psychiatric medication can also take days to wear off, so sometimes we celebrate healing too soon if we go off medicine and realise later there is a 'cliff', resulting in a major relapse.
- Medication often has side effects and can lead to some level of addiction. The same spiritual criteria we use for deciding on medicine for other illnesses should apply here.
- There are many testimonies of great recoveries and healing when all the resources provided by God, including medication under professional guidance, were exercised discerningly by the gospel community through their specific gifts and calling.

God is Able to Do More than We Can Think or Imagine
Let me conclude with a testimony. When I was serving as a missionary, we worked in Papua New Guinea with the Umanakaina and Daga tribal language groups.

There was a literacy supervisor we had trained called Livingstone. He did excellent work and evangelised to many as well. However, he became insane suddenly and was seen at the provincial town (120 km from our village). He was dirty, had unkempt long hair and nails, smelled rank and would chase people at the shops while mumbling to himself. The Umanakaina Christians were so discouraged and ashamed. We felt so devastated and helpless as he did not allow anyone to go close to him. For six years we would see him when we had to go to Alotau town. Non-Christians mocked the Christians.

Then in 2002, during a sports meet at a village where Umanakaina Christians had hiked over to (four mountains away from Umanakaina), Livingstone appeared at the front of our village house! No one could explain how he navigated 120 km of treacherous mountain, jungle and river trails; which strong local trekkers take over a week to complete, and turned up at our house where he had never been to before. We took the opportunity to pray for him. At one point, he became sane for a while and explained what had happened. Then he reverted to mumbling. However, what he told us helped us to pray more precisely. There was no noticeable change but we decided to cut his hair and nails, and we gave him a bath before dressing him in new clothes since he was compliant at the time.

He remained amongst us for a few months and during that time, he gradually started to make conversation, i.e. he was able to tell the time and day of the week, etc. He also started cleaning himself and taking baths. He then left with some of the Umanakaina people and went back to Alotau town.

The last time I saw him was in 2004. I found him sitting at a café in Alotau with a Bible in his hand, looking neat, well-dressed, well-mannered and talking with others. He said he often went there to meet people during their meals to share Christ to them. I did notice that at times, he seemed to be talking to himself. But then, at times so do I.

Daniel Jesudason
Chairman
Singapore Centre for Global Missions

THE DISCERNMENT SHEPHERDS NEED

– *Reflection* –

Shepherds tend to their sheep's wounds and needs. But shepherds have their own wounds and needs too.

Shepherds therefore need discernment. Discernment on how to tend to the wounds and needs of others and themselves.

These precious stories of pastoral care workers—God's shepherds—teach me a few things about discernment.

Discerning Mental Brokenness
Shepherds need wisdom to discern when a person has a mental condition or illness. That person may be a church member, cell group member or the shepherd himself or herself.

Pastor Seng Lee wrote about how some Christians have been wrongly told by their pastoral leaders that their condition is attention-seeking behaviour, caused by faithlessness or non-medical reasons. This is dangerous. Imagine telling someone who may have lung cancer that her incessant coughing is caused by a lack of faith.

Daniel Jesudason wrote about the need to discern when people are experiencing mental, physical, emotional and/or spiritual issues; and to refer them to professional help accordingly.

In this sense, pastoral workers are like medical general practitioners. They must be able to pick up on symptoms and address the issues holistically. They must direct the person to specialist care if needed. To do this, they must know enough about the types of issues that people go through; whether it's relational, financial, workplace-related, medical, emotional, mental, theological, spiritual or otherwise.

Just as doctors need to constantly learn about new medical issues, pastoral workers need to constantly equip themselves on understanding mental health issues, as well as many other issues.

Pastor Seng Lee's efforts in roping in professional psychiatrists and therapists to teach his church's pastoral teams, holding mental health talks for his church and weaving in mental health stories and issues over the pulpit; are great examples for many of us.

It is a huge challenge. I respect the many pastoral workers who take on this challenge with intentionality and diligence. We must support and encourage them for taking on this work.

Discerning Helpful and Unhelpful Approaches

Shepherds need wisdom to discern ways that help people in their mental brokenness, and ways that may be unhelpful or even do harm.

Every person's journey is different. Daniel Jesudason wrote about various different incidents with very different outcomes. There is no formula to helping people.

However, the stories present common threads of what are generally helpful. Soo-Inn, Pastor Seng Lee and Daniel Jesudason wrote about getting professional psychiatric treatment, medication and counselling.

Soo-Inn wrote about people who simply listened to him in his depression without dispensing suggestions or solutions. He wrote about people who were "just there with [him]" and "there for [him]", and the "many who prayed" for him. There were also those who gave practical help like taking his sons to tuition or the movies.

Likewise, Pastor Seng Lee wrote: "Love is best expressed through spending time listening to them".

We cannot all be psychiatrists or counsellors. But we can all be present with, and listen, to people who are hurting.

Discerning the Spiritual and the Physiological

Shepherds need to 'discern the spirits' (1 Corinthians 12:10), as it were.

Daniel Jesudason's stories show us that while medical and professional help is necessary, there is sometimes more than meets the eye.

As Christians, we cannot deny that there are spiritual forces at work in this world. To deal with issues holistically, we must employ all means to journey with those who are mentally broken. So it would not do well to only pray and deny medical treatment. It would also not do well to simply pop pills, but not pray and come alongside to be present and listen.

While shepherds tend to others, shepherds may suffer the 'hungry baker' problem and neglect tending to themselves.

The stories of Soo-Inn and Pastor Andre show me that pastoral workers are just as vulnerable to mental brokenness as any of us.

Soo-Inn fell into clinical depression and thankfully discerned the symptoms such that he reached out for help and sought psychiatric treatment and counselling.

Pastor Andre plunged into a crisis before he discerned that he needed the discipline of observing certain spiritual practices to help care for his own soul. These include setting aside a day for intentional rest and slowing down.

Pastor Seng Lee also exhorted us to "press the 'pause' button" and take care of ourselves so we can take care of others.

This applies to not only pastoral workers but to all of us. We all need to slow down, sabbath, rest and reflect. We need to take time out to be present before God and others so that we can discern our own physical, emotional, mental and spiritual health.

Discerning Community

Finally, shepherds do not only deal with individual sheep. They tend to a whole community.

Pastoral leaders have a role to discern the culture and practices of their church community, and to shape the culture and practices towards mental and emotional wellness. As

Pastor Andre wrote, mental and emotional health are tied to spiritual maturity. If we want a spiritually mature church, we must build mental and emotional health.

Pastor Seng Lee does this by holding mental health talks and seminars for his church. Pastor Andre does this by teaching about developing spiritual practices that build mental and emotional health, and this has borne fruit in transforming his church community to become more authentic about their emotional and mental struggles.

Soo-Inn's story of a mentoring group member who witnessed him in his depression shows me that such authenticity deepens community.

A community deeper in one another's lives is a community that depends further on God. Such a community witnesses to one another about their brokenness and the grace they receive from God, mediated through the lives and deeds of other members. Such a community becomes the good news to one another. Such a community witnesses to the world of the good news they live out in Christ.

That is a gospel community. God's power is indeed made perfect in weakness.

Ronald JJ Wong
Covenant Chambers LLC

JOURNEYING WITH THE MENTALLY ILL: A CHRISTIAN PERSPECTIVE

– *Afterword* –

When I was asked to contribute a chapter to this book, my initial thought was that I needed to consider a scientific or evidence-based response in order to be relevant. However, as I considered the topic at hand—of mental illness and the Church—I am struck by how the topic is framed.

For a long time, mental illness has been misinterpreted by the Church. If anything, many mental illnesses have been misconstrued to have spiritual and religious origins.[1] Psychiatry on the other hand, has often considered religious beliefs and practice as a symptom of mental illness. In fact, famous psychiatrists such as Sigmund Freud even thought of religion as a form of universal obsessional neurosis.[2] The incompatibility of these two topics appears to be stark, much like how science and superstition cannot stand side by side. If so, how do I make sense of the fact that I am both a psychiatrist and a Christian?

---

1 Deborah Cornah, *The impact of spirituality on mental health: a review of the literature* (London: Mental Health Foundation, 2006), https://www.mentalhealth.org.uk/sites/default/files/impact-spirituality.pdf.

2 Peter Gay, "ed.", *The Freud Reader* (New York, New York: W. W. Norton & Co., 1995), 435.

I was raised as a Christian all my life, brought to church by my mother even though my father did not attend Sunday services. I was baptised as an infant and spent many hours in church every week, whether it was Sunday school or watching my mother practice in the choir as I played with the pastor's children. I took my religion more seriously when I entered university and studied medicine.

I met several doctors who were accomplished and held on to their religious views fervently. I also met several Christian psychiatrists, the most prominent being Dr John White, who was both a psychiatrist as well as an evangelist with the International Fellowship of Evangelical Students. They all shaped my view that the medical approach to psychiatry made mental illness no different from physical illness. Over the years, in my practice of psychiatry, I also continued to grow in my faith and my conclusion is this—they are not incompatible at all.

As a Christian psychiatrist, I believe that God is sovereign in all things and that all illnesses, whether physical or mental, exist as a part of our fallen world. As medicine developed over time, we have identified ways of grouping symptoms together to define and understand illnesses.
As one practitioner describes, "disease" is the description of the cause of a pathological process involving the body—a description of what is happening to us.[3] Let's take leprosy as an example. As a "disease", it is described as being "caused by a bacteria that results in a loss of the ability to feel pain, with extensive skin lesions".

---

3   Marshall Marinker, "Why make people patients?," *Journal of Medical Ethics* 1, (1975), 81–84.

On the other hand, "illness" is understood as the personal experience of disease. In the case of leprosy, it is associated with much stigma and can sometimes be seen as a curse or punishment from God.

Finally, "sickness" is the role that the diseased person takes. In ancient societies where there is no cure for leprosy, the victims are banished from the community because of the infectious nature of the disease.

The same can be said of mental illnesses such as schizophrenia and depression. There are specific symptoms that determine these illnesses. The problem lies in our inability to identify specific pathological processes in this point in time. We know it has to do with the complex neural networks in our brains, but we have not been able to pinpoint the problem and completely contain the symptoms although medications have been developed to ameliorate the symptoms and improve the patient's functioning.

As the cause of mental illnesses are not clear, the symptoms also lend themselves to misconceptions. Unfortunately, typical symptoms of schizophrenia are hallucinations and delusions. Hallucinations refer to false perceptions that patients have of the world around them. They can see, hear and experience perceptual abnormalities that others cannot. If a person with mental illness is religious, he may hear someone talking to him and may draw the conclusion that it is the voice of God speaking to him. Delusions are false beliefs held with utter conviction that defy logic. Often these have either a paranoid (someone is trying to harm them) or a grandiose (there is a special power endowed on the person) nature and again can be misinterpreted as a religious experience.

I believe that God can sanctify us in the midst of suffering and pain. Just as God can heal physical illness like leprosy, he can heal mental ones as well. Similarly, if God can allow leprosy to befall a person (even a great king like Uzziah as written in 2 Kings 15 and 2 Chronicles 26), He can also allow mental illness to take place (see the example of King Nebuchadnezzar in Daniel 4).

Finally, I think that God has a purpose for each one of us and sends us to do his work. As I continue in my psychiatric practice, I regularly try to bring a spiritual perspective to the recovery of my patients who have mental illnesses. In Asian psychiatric practice, accepting the role of religion in helping patients is an important domain in the recovery of illness. As many mental illnesses such as anxiety, depression and schizophrenia are chronic illnesses; there is a need to help the patient cope better with the condition. Let me share some principles that have been of assistance in my almost 30 years of working with the mentally ill.

How Can We Use Our Christian Values to Help People Suffering from Mental Illness?

We should not be afraid of asking about the spiritual needs of someone with a mental illness. We should in fact ask about the positive aspects of life that give them meaning, hope, value and purpose.

When needed, we should not hinder persons and their families from seeking spiritual support. I find it worrying when doctors want nothing to do with speaking with a pastor because its not 'scientific'. Spiritual support is critical in any illness. It allows a safe space for patients to pray, meditate or worship even in the hospital. At the Institute of Mental Health, we have a room that has been dedicated for this purpose. I believe that we should form links, connections or networks amongst community groups or agencies, so that support can be provided when needed. More importantly, we must not dismiss or ignore spiritual experiences even though someone has a mental illness. However, I do remain sensitive and draw the line, so as not to been misunderstood as proselytizing to someone who is suffering against their will.

How Can We Tell the Difference between Religious Experience and Mental Illness?

Mental illness is distressful and not life enriching at all. A religious experience should be positive and purposeful. I often suggest that families approach a pastor for assistance before seeing a psychiatrist as pastors are the 'experts' in spiritual experiences, whereas psychiatrists are correspondingly, experts in mental illnesses. If a person's behaviour is inconsistent with religious practice and experience, it is more likely to be a mental illness. At the same time, as mental illnesses have consistent symptoms drawn up in the standard classification systems such as the International Classification of Diseases from World Health Organisation and the American Psychiatric Association's Diagnostic Statistical Manual, this can be used as a clear reference as well.

When Should We Seek Professional Help?

Mental health professionals are not common in Singapore. They include psychiatrists, clinical psychologists, psychiatric social workers, as well as counsellors. One should seek help when it becomes clear that the individual affected is not developing appropriately despite all the support provided. For instance, the individual may be causing persistent distress to himself and those who are close to him. It becomes increasingly apparent that his behaviour is affecting his daily life, and functioning at a personal, relational and occupational perspective is affected.

Although a chronic illness may not be curable, symptoms can be improved and situations will become better with the potential of treatment. Today, I dare say that we have many human interventions to make lives better and the treatment of mental illnesses is much more recovery oriented.

Concluding Thoughts

I believe that our understanding of mental illnesses have been divorced from our understanding physical illnesses for far too long. This stigma against mental illness has affected how our Christian communities have treated those with mental illnesses. The tide is changing as professional organisations are seeing the value of religion in the care of the mentally ill, and churches are improving their awareness and understanding of mental illnesses and the needs of those who are suffering and in need of healing.

A caring and recovery-oriented approach towards mental illnesses is needed, and there is a need to form stronger networks of care to support the mentally ill - networks which bring both the churches and hospitals together to work for a common good.

A/Prof Daniel Fung
Chairman Medical Board
Institute of Mental Health, Singapore

ACKNOWLEDGEMENTS

This book was a collaborative effort, made possible only by the gifts of time and labour from many generous volunteers. The editors would especially like to thank:

Micah Singapore, for spearheading this second book of the *Good News for Bruised Reeds* series, in their tireless endeavour to build up the Singapore Church in matters of social justice.

Each of our writers, some of whom bravely revisited painful memories to provide us with these powerful testimonies. Thank you for giving us glimpses into your worlds, and for trusting us with your stories.

Leow Wen Pin, for his incisive theological overview; *Tan Soo-Inn*, *Jonathon Cho* and *Ronald JJ Wong* for their insightful reflections at the end of each section.

Emma Lee from Awaken Studio, for our beautiful book cover illustration.

The team at *Graceworks* for their publishing expertise and the careful work that went into preparing the manuscript.

Mariel Chee, *Sophie Cheng*, *Jonathan Cho*, *Jethro Leong*, *Sharon Mah*, *Michelle Tan*, *Ronald JJ Wong* and *Ethel Yap*, for contributing their many talents to the book launch.

Finally, we thank the Lord for His grace that sustained us through this project, and for the hope that He alone provides to the bruised reeds in this world.

HELP RESOURCES IN SINGAPORE

TELEPHONIC HELPLINES

Institute of Mental Health (IMH) Helpline

This IMH helpline is for anyone experiencing any mental health crisis, or who needs to help someone who is experiencing a mental health crisis.

Contact: (+65) 6389 2222 (24 hours)
Website: https://www.imh.com.sg/
Address: Buangkok Green Medical Park
10 Buangkok View
Singapore 539747

Singapore Association of Mental Health (SAMH) Counselling Helpline

This helpline offers information and assistance on mental health matters and psychological issues.

Contact: 1800 283 7019 (Mondays to Fridays, 9 a.m. to 6 p.m., except public holidays)
Website: https://www.samhealth.org.sg/about-samh/contact-us/
Address: Block 139 Potong Pasir Avenue 3
#01-136, Singapore 350139

Samaritans of Singapore (SOS) Hotline

This hotline offers emotional support for individuals who are contemplating suicide, affected by another's suicide or are having difficulty coping in a crisis.

Contact: 1800 221 4444 (24 hours)
Email: pat@sos.org.sg

Lifeline NUS
This lifeline is for NUS students who are experiencing life threatening psychological emergencies, such as: suicidal thoughts, severe panic or anxiety attacks, trauma or mental disorientation from any recent emotionally distressing event.

Contact: **(+65) 6516 7777 (24 hours)**

COUNSELLING SERVICES

Arting Hearts
Arting Hearts provides clinical art therapy for clients with mental health issues. It offers therapy with a range of art materials and mediums (clay work, paints, textiles, crafts etc.), both in individual and group sessions. Each session is facilitated by a professional art therapist, and aims to improve the emotional and mental wellness of the client. Arting Hearts welcomes clients of all ages, and no prior art experience is necessary.

Website: **http://artinghearts.sg**
Email: **someone@artinghearts.sg**
Contact Person: **Veon Lim, Art Psychotherapist, MA, AThR**
Contact: **(+65) 8711 9227**
Address: **195 Pearl's Hill Terrace #02-21, Singapore 168976**

Christian Counselling Singapore
Christian Counselling comprises a team of Christian professional counsellors who provide Bible based Counselling Services. They minister to clients who are suffering from depression.

Website: **http://christiancounsellingsingapore.com/**

Email: **info@olivebranch.com.sg**
Contact: **(+65) 8322 8861**
Address: **229 Mountbatten Road**
Mountbatten Square #02-32
Singapore 398007

Focus on the Family Singapore
Life can be overwhelming and relationships can get strained when there are issues that are seemingly impossible to resolve. Yet, everyone has a voice and deserves to be heard. Focus on the Family Singapore offers hope and support through counselling for individuals, married couples and families. Be it depression, marital conflicts or other family challenges, their counsellors are committed to journey with you.

Website: **https://family.org.sg/counseling**
Contact: **(+65) 6491 0700**
Address: **9 Bishan Place, #08-03**
Junction 8 Office Tower
Singapore 579837

Wesley Methodist Church Counselling Services
Wesley Counselling Services provides both Christian and non-religious counselling for clients who are struggling with depression, suicidal thoughts and anxiety. They are recognised by and listed in the NCSS Directory of Social Services.

Website: **https://wesleymc.org/counselling**
Contact Person: **Caroline Ong, (Monday to Friday, 9 a.m. to 6 p.m.)**
Contact: **(+65) 6837 9214**
Address: **5 Fort Canning Road**
Singapore 179493

MENTAL HEALTH COMMUNITIES AND SUPPORT GROUPS

Caregivers Alliance Limited (CAL)
CAL is a professional non-profit organisation that provides support to caregivers of persons with mental health issues. They offer education, support networks, crisis support, tailored services and self-care enablement.

Website: https://www.cal.org.sg
Contact: (+65) 6460 4400
Helpline: (+65) 6388 8631
Address: 491-B River Valley Road
#04-04 Valley Point Office Tower
Singapore 248373

Psaltcare Depression and Bipolar Support Groups
Psaltcare runs various peer-led support groups to strengthen and sustain the recovery of individuals with mental health conditions. Their DBSA (Depression and Bipolar Support Alliance) Peer Support Groups are open to anyone who is recovering from Depression, Bipolar and/or Anxiety disorder, or other mental health challenges. Their Christian Peer Support Group reaches out to those who want to include prayer, Bible reading, and worship as part of their recovery into wholeness. Both groups are facilitated by trained Peer Support specialists who are in a good state of recovery from their mental health conditions.

Website:http://www.psaltcare.com/peer-support-services/dbsa-peer-support-group/
Address: 10 Sinaran Drive
#11-16 Novena Medical Centre
Singapore 307506

Resilience Collective

Resilience Collective is a community where persons in recovery from mental health or trauma are empowered to build resilience. It is a platform for persons in recovery to co-develop workshops and other initiatives for the mental health community. It allows peers to network with like-minded people, to give and receive support, and explore the shared purpose of building resilience together. Resilience Collective also organises outreach to build up the community's understanding of important wellness and recovery topics.

Website: **https://www.resilience.org.sg/**
Email: **contactus@resilience.org.sg**

GRACEWORKS

Graceworks is a publishing and training consultancy based in Singapore, dedicated to promoting spiritual friendship in church and society, and seeing lives transformed through books that present truth for life.

Our publications can be found on our online store, *www.graceworks.com.sg/store*. Paperbacks are also available on Bookdepository and Amazon. eBooks on Kindle, iBooks and Kobo. You can contact us at *enquiries@graceworks.com.sg*, or follow us on Facebook (@GraceworksSG) and Instagram (graceworkssg).

Micah Singapore is an organic community and coalition of Christ followers, ministries and churches passionate about seeking shalom through justice, mercy and integral mission.

Find out more at *https://www.micahsingapore.org/*.

www.ingramcontent.com/pod-product-compliance
Lightning Source LLC
LaVergne TN
LVHW041939070526
838199LV00051BA/2841